Jane Paech grew up on a farm in South Australia, where her lifelong love of food was born. Living in New York further ignited her passion for both food and travel, and when an opportunity to live in Paris arose, she turned from a career in nursing to travel writing, unable to resist documenting all the wonderful sights, smells and tastes she discovered. Her work has been featured in various publications including *Australian Gourmet Traveller* and *Qantas* inflight magazine. She is the author of *A Family in Paris: Stories of food, life and adventure*, published by Lantern, which won the Australian category for Food Literature at the prestigious Gourmand World Cookbook Awards in 2012. This is her second book. Jane blogs at knifeandforkintheroad.wordpress.com

♦

Delicious
Days in
PARIS

Walking tours to explore the city's food and culture

JANE PAECH

LANTERN

an imprint of
PENGUIN BOOKS

CHAPTER ONE

A Glass of
VIN
NATUREL

◆◆◆

I snap shut the windows, button my coat, and rattle down the stairs into the fresh Paris morning. At the café on the corner, I stop for a *crème* and croissant and write up a few notes. It's warm and bustling with the comforting murmur of voices. From my window seat on Rue Saint-Antoine, I look out on the continuous flow of pedestrians and watch the rhythm and routine of a Paris morning. Bikes whizz by, bells ringing, as workers rush towards the steps of the Saint Paul metro station. Two little girls bundled in coats walk hand in hand with their mother, schoolbags bouncing on their backs, gloves swinging from their strings.

One of the things I most love about Paris is that it's a great walking city: compact, easy to navigate and breathtakingly beautiful. Back in Australia I'd succumbed to the suburban car culture, and I had forgotten the buzz that comes from clicking open a heavy door and being instantly in touch with a vibrant city. To make the most of Paris, however, it is wise to arrive in a fit state. Naturally integrating walking into your day allows you to indulge, guilt-free, in all those divine pastries and chocolates you bump into along the way. It also means you discover so many things you would not have otherwise.

A French verb I find intriguing is *flâner. Un flâneur* is a stroller, someone who mooches through city streets, footloose and fancy-free with little agenda. But it's more than this, for there is logic to the haphazardness of the walk. The point is to leave yourself alert to chance encounters and unforeseen discoveries. The French *flâneur* does not stride with purpose, but experiences the ramble with the sole aim of pleasure. The word also implies pause for reflection. *Un flâneur* stops to smell the roses at the florist on the corner; they are keen voyeurs and detached observers of life. Travellers, I believe, benefit from taking on the characteristics of *un flâneur*. There is such joy in surrendering to the city and cherishing the moment, perhaps even stumbling upon a secret spot. Take what you need from a guidebook, but be sure to sample life as well as chocolate, and make your own memories. I like to think of myself as *une flâneuse*. Walking is also when I generate ideas. This trip, however, I also have an agenda. I brush the crumbs from my lap, button my coat once more and start walking towards Place de la Bastille. Eastern Paris is really opening up and low rents have seen an influx of young Parisians in recent years. Jam-packed with innovative bistros and edgy wine bars, it is an exciting and different part of the city to explore, far from classical Paris.

A block past Opéra Bastille on Avenue Daumesnil I climb three stories up a brick and stone stairwell that leads to a landscaped path. I set off, walking under a series of trellises flanked with trees and plants. Today, it's somewhat devoid of greenery and colour but in spring and summer one can have the feeling of momentarily rambling down a country lane past fragrant climbing roses, honeysuckle and lavender, and at the next turn being lost in a green jungle of bamboo. In summertime the path is shaded by linden, maple and flowering cherry trees, and a duck or two glide on the rectangular ponds. Children play along the pathway, joggers pound by and park benches offer a unique place to read and picnic, or simply sit and ponder.

Treasured and guarded by the locals in this emerging part of town, La Promenade Plantée is one of Paris's best-kept secrets. Also known as *La Coulée Verte,* the walkway is the world's first elevated urban park, on which New York City's popular High Line was modelled. It's a fascinating example of the creative use of abandoned infrastructure, turning an inner-city eyesore into a stroll in the country. Originally a railroad track, the trail follows the route of the former Vincennes line that extended to the south-eastern suburbs of Paris. The line was shut down in 1969 and by the early 1990s the track was completely transformed into this intriguing use of public space. Stretching 4.5 kilometres to the Bois de Vincennes, a sprawling public park on the eastern edge of the city, the Promenade Planteé runs almost the entire width of the 12th arrondissement. This morning, however, I am only walking a portion of the path, the elevated section running for 1.5 kilometres to the Jardin de Reuilly, a good halfway stopping point along the green belt. The reason? Lunch.

La Promenade
Plantée

As I walk, it's the changing vistas and the engaging new perspective on Paris the promenade offers that I find most interesting. Along with glimpses of the city's skyline, you can observe eastern Paris in an up-close and personal way. At this distance one can spy through windows and study gorgeous wrought-iron balconies. I imagine it's like viewing eastern Paris from the vantage point of a beady-eyed city pigeon, soaring almost at the level of cathedral spires and treetops, sloping slate roofs and chimneypots. On the corner of Rue de Rambouillet there is a most unusual sight. The top of the 12th arrondissement's police station is adorned with twelve caryatids – reproductions of Michelangelo's *The Dying Slave.* The original statue is housed in the Louvre.

Beneath me on Avenue Daumesnil, the red brick arches of the former railroad viaduct have also been restored and transformed

into the Viaduc des Arts, a succession of art and design studios and bespoke craft workshops, stretching to the Jardin de Reuilly. Occasional stairways down to the street provide access to nip down and browse. There are all sorts of unusual wares and specialists here, from made-to-order parasols and a paper embosser to a producer of mechanical dolls and songbirds. These workshops are really the kinds of places locals make a deliberate journey to; you won't trip over these treasures by chance, but the detour is worth it.

Before long, I arrive at the Jardin de Reuilly and rest for a while. Formerly a freight train station, today it is an expansive grassed area with a raised footbridge, a series of landscaped walkways, nude female statues and a rose garden. In a little wooden hut, a fountain offers free chilled sparkling water. It is connected to the public water system, and thirsty walkers have a choice between *eau gazeuse* or *eau non gazeuse*. The French are known for their high consumption of bottled water and the experiment is an attempt to both promote Paris tap water, and wean Parisians from plastic bottles. A man arrives with a shopping trolley full of coloured glass bottles and fills them one by one with sparkling water.

From here, I wander off the promenade and through the lesser-known streets of the 12th towards my lunch destination – about a twenty-minute walk. By the time I turn left on to the long Rue de Reuilly, a soft, steady rain has set in. I could take the metro; it's two direct stops from Montgallet station to Faidherbe-Chaligny, but I don't mind Paris in the rain, it heightens the senses – unless it's really bucketing down. Rain has its charms and drawbacks, as does every season in Paris. Soon, however, my umbrella is almost redundant as large drops splash my new Parisian boots. Water drips from the awnings in loud lines. It's bucketing down. I'm grateful to swing open the door at Le Bistrot Paul Bert and enter its warm glow. I throw my dripping umbrella in with the others,

La Promenade
Plantée

making a mental note to remember it on the way out. I have lost count of the wet umbrellas I've forgotten at restaurants and left on metros over the years.

◇◇◇◇◇

My lunch mate, the American Wendy Lyn, is at the bar when I arrive, chatting to the owner, Bertrand Aboyneau. This lively 'Southern gal' who calls Paris home has a delicious life that revolves around eating and drinking. Strings to her bow include working for many years as an international public relations and restaurant consultant to some of the best chefs and restaurants in the world, and launching the first USA Michelin Red Guide. Wendy is the author of *The Paris Kitchen*, a culinary blog chock-full of Paris hotspots as well as some perennial favourites. It's especially worth checking out if you're after an up-to-the-minute wine bar or popular neo-bistro. But it's Wendy's intimate foodie walking tours of vibrant Paris neighbourhoods, with tastings, *bien sûr*, that really bring the city alive for visitors. Scrumptious hors d'oeuvres to the Paris food scene that connect travellers to premium produce and showcase the best of regional France. Occasionally, Wendy also offers her Kitchen Confidential series. Privileged participants are given a one-off opportunity to step behind the scenes into the restaurant kitchens, workshops and cellars of renowned chefs and artisans.

Le Paul Bert is one of Wendy's favourite haunts and we sit and talk food over a bottle of Touraine la Tesnière. At the next table, a group of boisterous old men is tucking into *terrine de campagne*. She motions to a couple in the corner. 'They come in every day,' she beams. With a true bistro spirit, and decorated

Le Bistrot
Paul Bert

I love Paris in the springtime
I love Paris in the fall
I love Paris in the summer
when it sizzles
I love Paris in the winter
when it drizzles
I love Paris every moment
Every moment of the year.

COLE PORTER

with flea-market finds, the sepia-toned Le Paul Bert is where locals and an international crowd congregate for a juicy rare steak and a few glasses of *vin rouge*. A blackboard menu scrawled with bistro classics is propped on a chair next to us, and on the wall are the specials, including a *Côte de bœuf béarnaise pour 2 personnes*.

While Le Paul Bert is your typical neighbourhood bistro serving Gallic grub, it also represents a new breed of the old-style bistro in that Aboyneau is serious about quality and ensures produce is carefully sourced. His *steak-frites* are among the best in town and the impressive list of *les vins naturels* (organic and biodynamic wines) favours small producers with a high regard for *terroir*. And then there is that fabulous cheese tray I spied within seconds of entering the place, topped with a prudently selected assortment of oozing *fromage*.

Along with quality produce, part of the attraction is the bistro's authenticity, which draws locals like Wendy. There is nothing spectacular about the place, but simultaneously, it's everything a great bistro should be: busy, crowded and noisy, with ageless décor and good food and wine. Diners are jammed together and harried waiters stride over the cracked-tile floor. Often, Wendy explains, travellers have the wrong idea of what a classic French bistro should be, and your expectations will influence whether you have a good or a bad dining experience. Bistros are not restaurants, nor should you expect the same kind of ambience or service. Don't, for example, expect the rules to be bent when it comes to substituting or changing elements

Le Bistrot
Paul Bert

of a dish. Also, 'If you want the waiter's attention, you will most likely have to speak up,' says Wendy. 'It's just the way it is.' These differences are, ultimately, what make Paris Paris. It's part of the charm, like the timeless décor in old-school French bistros.

Ambience, however, isn't everything, and while atmospheric old-style bistros with good, honest, traditional French cooking still exist, finding them can sometimes be like stepping between the raindrops. In the past decade, the culinary landscape has also changed in myriad exciting new ways and the city continues to redefine itself. Inspiring gastronomic choices are popping up like *les parapluies* (umbrellas) in the rain. 'Bistronomy', a term coined to describe a posse of well-trained young chefs who turned their backs on careers in starred kitchens to open neo-bistros with high-quality, creative cuisine at affordable prices, continues to evolve and take bistro classics to a new place.

As Wendy cuts through her rare steak in a creamy cognac sauce, she says that the places doing well on the Paris gastronomic scene are small with good food – addresses such as Frenchie as well as Spring and Septime, with pedigree produce and short, interesting menus. 'To explain the phenomenon, we're talking eighteen chairs, not eighteen tables,' says Wendy. 'Organic, well-sourced products and heirloom vegetables are in, fussy is out.' Local, natural and artisanal are prevalent themes, with a focus on flavour. The trend is also for exclusive breeds and menus that declare the origins of produce. Some producers have become 'star suppliers', with products such as Jean-Yves Bordier's butter, Eric Kayser's bread, and meat from celebrated butcher Hugo Desnoyer almost reaching cult status. There is a new respect for vegetables and more interesting choices are now available.

Clamouring for a seat in the more popular neo-bistros, however, can be tough. If you're keen to reserve a table, do it as soon as you've booked your flight to Paris, because some have become so sought-after they are almost impossible to get in to. When there are so many dining options in Paris, part of me thinks, 'Why bother reserving weeks, even months ahead for the sort of creative modern fare we do well at home?' Well, firstly, there is still a very French flavour about these powerful foodie magnets. Secondly, as well as experiencing what's hot on the culinary scene you get to enjoy a gastronomic meal in a relaxed bistro ambience, which translates to excellent value for money. The food cooked by these gifted chefs is flawless but not fussy: an appealing mix of sophisticated technique, and simplicity and naturalness on the plate. 'For this younger generation of chefs, the focus is on the food more than the décor,' says Wendy. 'There is less obsessive interest in haute cuisine. We need more places like this in Paris and more, thankfully, are on the way. It's what people want, and what they are responding to.'

Some of these young chefs are part of a movement called Le Fooding, a portmanteau of the words 'food' and 'feeling'. The term was invented in 2000 by French food journalist Alexandre Cammas and inspired a new generation to dare to be different. These chefs aim to melt the rigid corners of French dining and do away with the stuffiness. Considering themselves as artisans, they reject rules in favour of ability and *liberté*. The term Le Fooding also applies to a contemporary restaurant guide. It's the Michelin Guide's younger, hipper cousin and highlights talented, forward-thinking chefs who do not necessarily have Michelin stars.

'The other big trend is *le vin naturel*,' continues my culinary concierge as I watch a Paris Brest whizz by: an absolute classic of a French dessert involving a thick wheel of *pâte à choux* sandwiching a puff of praline pastry cream. 'France is a world leader in natural wines but because they don't travel well, it's difficult to get your hands on them outside of France.' A visit to Paris is therefore a good opportunity to sample them. 'Wine bars are a good opportunity to sample them. 'Wine bars are huge at the moment,' says Wendy. 'A lot of bistros are setting up wine bars at the end of the street, around the corner, as annexes to their main addresses.' Auboyneau has recently opened Le 6 Paul Bert a few

doors down from his bistro. The wine bar with *épicerie* (grocery) offers diners simple but inventive dishes and is already creating quite a buzz. Le Comptoir's Yves Camdeborde has L'Avant Comptoir, where chefs and people from the food industry come for a plate of *jambon* and a glass of wine; it's a tiny, stand-up space, which makes it fun. Frenchie's *bar à vins*, winner of the best wine bar in the Prix Fooding Guide 2012, is across the street.

This new breed of *bars à vins* often combines a grocery where you can buy excellent quality regional produce with a cellar and eatery. A sharing platter of cheese and charcuterie or a board of *saucisson sec* or *jambon au pays Basque* is a great way to sample well-sourced French produce and vibrant natural wine from artisan producers. Even the famous wine store Les Caves Augé, known for its tradition of excellence, has embraced *le vin naturel*. Like the neo-bistro, however, natural wines have their devotees and critics, and unfined and unfiltered wines are not to everyone's taste.

On our way out, Wendy shows me the fish house next door, L'Ecailler du Bistrot. It has charm in spades, bucketed in from Brittany. Inside, sturdy striped serviettes are folded across each place setting; there's a fun, nautical atmosphere with maritime objects scattered about the wood-panelled dining room. 'You'd be hard pressed to find the catch of the day fresher than this at such moderate prices,' says Wendy. The bistro is the seafood annex of Le Paul Bert. The board outside tempts passers-by with a dozen oysters du Bélon and half a lobster with *frites*. I farewell Wendy and peek into Le Chardenoux on the corner, a traditional bistro with turn-of-the-century décor, and a reliable old favourite serving updated French classics. A gastronomic little stretch indeed! Just a couple of streets over, Aussie chef James Henry continues the theme with his new hipster hotspot Bones Bar & Restaurant. Formerly of Spring, Henry more recently made a splash in town while manning the stoves at Au Passage, a cool wine bar in eastern Paris.

My mind whirls with possibilities as I wander back to my friends' apartment in the Marais. Paris never ceases to surprise and delight me. At every turn I find *un frisson* of excitement, another French word I love, meaning, in this sense, a momentary thrill. The Paris food scene now offers more dining options and a wider range of experiences than ever before. Interestingly, many of the *chefs du moment* are from out of town. There are exceptionally good restaurants for every budget, taste and occasion; it's a wonderful mix of trend and tradition, from the neo-bistro to the traditional French bistro to the glamour of a Michelin-starred meal. There is also a growing variety of good ethnic places including Moroccan, Vietnamese, Thai and Indian. Then of course there are those rich French pastries to devour at an indulgent afternoon tea; and chocolate shops, scrumptious food tours, and markets to explore in search of picnic fare. I'd better get my skates on. Rain starts to fall. *Zut*! I have forgotten my umbrella, *encore*! I'll just have to step between the raindrops. ◊

La Crèmerie,
La Promenade
Plantée,
Chardenoux,
Le Marais

ADDRESSES

Le Bistrot Paul Bert
18, Rue Paul Bert, 75011
☎ 01 43 72 24 01

Bones Bar & Restaurant
43 Rue Godefroy Cavaignac, 75011
☎ 09 80 75 32 08
www.bonesparis.com

Le Chardenoux
1, Rue Jules Vallès, 75011
☎ 01 43 71 49 52

Le Comptoir du Relais & L'Avant Comptoir
9, Carrefour de l'Odéon, 75006
☎ 01 44 27 07 97
www.hotel-paris-relais-saint-germain.com

L'Ecailler du Bistrot
22, Rue Paul Bert, 75011
☎ 01 43 72 76 77

Frenchie (and wine bar across road)
5-6, Rue du Nil, 75002
☎ 01 40 39 96 19
www.frenchie-restaurant.com

Promenade Plantée
Entrance: intersection of Avenue Daumesnil and Avenue Ledru-Rollin, 75012
Open Mon–Fri 8 a.m. Weekends 9 a.m. Closes around dusk.

La Régalade
49, Avenue Jean Moulin, 75014
☎ 01 45 45 68 58
A gem tucked down in the 14th with an old-fashioned ambience and updated French bistro classics.

Septime
80, Rue de Charonne, 75011
☎ 01 43 67 38 29

Le 6 Paul Bert
6 Rue Paul Bert, 75011
☎ 01 43 79 14 32

Spring Restaurant
6, Rue Bailleul, 75001
☎ 01 45 96 05 72
www.springparis.fr
Spring also offers Grand Afternoon Tastings – wine-tasting classes in English with cheese and charcuterie. See website for details.

Le Viaduc des Arts
1-129, Avenue Daumesnil
www.leviaducdesarts.fr
For Wendy Lyn's Paris blog and details of her food tours visit:
www.thepariskitchen.com
www.lefooding.com

OTHER SPOTS TO TASTE NATURAL WINE

La Crèmerie
9, Rue des Quatre Vents, 75006
📞 01 43 54 99 30
www.lacremerie.fr
Dripping with charm, this
gorgeous little *bar à vin*
and bottle shop is housed in
a converted nineteenth-century
dairy.

Les Fines Gueules
43, Rue Croix des Petits Champ,
75001
📞 01 42 61 35 41
www.lesfinesgueules.fr

Au Passage
1b, Passage Saint-Sébastien,
75011
📞 01 43 55 07 52

CHAPTER TWO

Rose & Jasmine
MACARONS

♦♦♦

In the heart of the Right Bank is the refined 1ˢᵗ arrondissement, dominated by the Louvre Palace, a patchwork of elegant squares and sweeping formal gardens. Here you will find stunning vistas, gorgeous architecture and lashings of glamour. Chanel shopping bags rule the street, and designer dogs lounge on fashion-house floors. The neighbourhood, which slides like melted chocolate into the glitzy 8ᵗʰ, is classic Paris, both old and new. Luxury hotels plump up their pillows and grand gourmet emporiums offer a cornucopia of delights. The scent of perfume, hot chocolate and flowers lingers in the air, and lingerie stores seduce. Spend the day and spoil yourself – and be sure to indulge in a macaron or two along the way.

For an elegant introduction to this glossy part of town and to soak up the full splendour of Paris, start at the Cour Carrée at the eastern end of the Louvre Palace, with its grand splashing fountain. As you walk towards Pei's glass pyramid and on through the archway of the Place du Carrousel, a fabulous panorama slowly comes into view. You step into the Jardin des Tuileries, and suddenly it seems all of Paris is before you: a thrilling, uninterrupted vista of grand monuments and thoroughfares. Your eyes first climb the obelisk at Place de la Concorde before travelling down the Champs-Élysées through the majestic Arc de Triomphe, and all the way to the Grande Arche of La Défense. This spectacular line of sight is known as the *Axe Historique* or the Grand Axis of Paris.

No matter what the season, the Jardin des Tuileries is breathtakingly beautiful. In winter, the shivering bare trees are silhouetted against a grey sky that reflects in the ponds, resulting in a stark, ethereal beauty. As you crunch over the white gravel, breath swirling into the air, you feel as though you are walking through a washed-out watercolour. On this lovely sunny morning in late spring, the classic French park is dressed like an elegant model in cool green and adorned with masses of flowers that contrast with the azure-blue sky. Boules chink under the linden trees and Parisians promenade along its wide central pathway. On sunny Sundays, the whole of Paris comes out to play, and children sail toy boats on the pond.

I sit on a park bench and take in this splendid scene before crossing the gardens for lunch. Turning on to Rue Royale, a street dripping in history and glamour, I pass Maxim's, a Paris institution and supreme example of Art Nouveau, a flamboyant style of decorative art and architecture that drew inspiration from feminine charm and the natural world. The legendary restaurant is rather touristy, but upstairs, the lovely Musée Maxim's presents La Collection 1900. The museum is set up as an exquisite Art Nouveau apartment, furnished with masterpieces from the Belle Epoque collected by the famous couturier Pierre Cardin. There are sporadic guided tours in English.

Further up, a queue curls from the door of the famous tea salon, Ladurée, where plump cherubs bake bread on the ceiling. Oozing with style, it's the place to come for some of the best macarons in town and attracts a fashionable crowd, many of whom are taking *une petite pause* from shopping in the surrounding luxury boutiques. This green and gold chocolate box of a spot is also a *très* Parisian option for a light lunch, and the thick, silken *chocolat noir* will stay in your dreams. My chocoholic daughter Georgie rates it as her hands-down favourite hot chocolate in the city. If you're merely passing, grab a macaron at the counter to keep your energy up. Perennial classics include chocolate, raspberry, lemon, and salted-butter caramel.

The Louvre and Jardin des Tuileries

Across the road, I duck through Cité Berryer, an open-air pedestrian passageway that connects Rue Royale with Rue Boissy d'Anglas. Flanked by Dior, Gucci and Chanel, the fashionable thoroughfare is a fairyland at Christmastime, elegantly dressed in silver baubles from head to high-heeled toe. The *très chic* Le Village has prime position and a great people-watching terrace shaded by a sprawling white awning. Here, stick-thin women nibble on smoked salmon with wedges of lemon and sip sparkling water.

At the end of the passage, I cross the road to arrive at Bread & Roses. A delicious spot for a light, casual lunch, the emphasis is on fresh quality ingredients and simply prepared, wholesome dishes. On the menu is a Provençale tart with fig, zucchini, artichoke and goat's cheese; a *pissaladière*; and a Grande Salade of prawns, chicken, grapefruit, avocado and cherry tomatoes. I order the leek, goat's cheese and asparagus quiche, and with a glass of Chablis in hand, watch the desserts float by – a fresh raspberry tart, sticky-toffee pudding and a tangy *tarte au citron*. My scrumptious quiche arrives, crowned with luscious rounds of thick, creamy *chèvre.* Bread is organic and made in-house.

After lunch, I skirt quickly around Place de la Madeleine, home to the imposing Madeleine Church and a dress circle of gourmet stores, including two of the most esteemed in France. Kissed in lipstick pink, the grand food emporium Fauchon stretches over half a block. Its specialist counters offer one-stop luxury shopping, fabulous boxed delicacies to stash in your suitcase, and an

'Macarons only weigh a few grams, but that's enough to leave your senses quivering with pleasure. Their thin, crisp shell, slightly rounded shape, tempting colours and tender interiors draw devotees to devour them with their eyes, and caress their smooth surface. Their flavours solicit the nose and, when one bites into that crisp shell, the ears tingle with pleasure and the palate is finally rewarded.'

PIERRE HERMÉ

extensive selection of French wines and Champagne. Across the
square is Hédiard, striking in red and black stripes and bursting
with exotic fruits and bright vegetables, as well as jewel-hued
jams, rare teas and aromatic coffees. Long-time rivals, both stores
are equally decadent.

A precious-stone's throw away, Chanel wafts down Rue
Cambon from the flagship store. Coco lived in a suite at the Ritz
on the nearby Place Vendôme, an exclusive square edged in a glittering strand of jewellery stores. Her first fragrance, the timeless
Chanel No. 5, was launched in 1921 and the bottle was modelled
on the octagonal shape of Place Vendôme. Today, it is perhaps
the single most recognised women's fragrance in the world.

At the bottom of Rue Cambon, with accolades piled as high as
a macaron tower, is the Dior of desserts. Pierre Hermé is a genius
of pastry and most famous for his macarons. They come in subtle
colours and exciting flavours, with unusual combinations such
as lemon with caramelised fennel. He compares his ever-popular
Ispahan – a combination of rose macaron, rose-petal cream
flavoured with lychees, and fresh raspberries – to the classic Chanel
suit, and like a fashion designer, he releases themed seasonal
collections. Hermé's current collection, Les Jardins, will lead you
down the garden path in the best possible way. Each month he
launches a new gourmet experience based on the flavours and
perfumes of flowers and spices. I bite into 'Rose & Jasmine' and
hear that delicious pop.

From here, I spend the afternoon shopping in and around Rue
Saint-Honoré, a long luxurious ribbon that ties the 1st arrondissement together. I pass the spanking new Mandarin Oriental Hotel,
a thoroughly modern splash of Asian-inspired indulgence in a
prestigious location, and sneak into the glass-walled lobby for a
peek. Then just before Rue Castiglione, Porsches and convertibles
block the road outside the deluxe Hôtel Costes, an opulent address

with a trendy bar and courtyard café that attracts Paris's über-chic crowd. Equally alluring, however, is Roses Costes, the little florist on the footpath attached to the hotel. Especially for those who adore roses, it is one of the most enchanting boutiques in all of Paris, and there are *only* roses: buckets and bouquets of them. Blooms are strewn on the floor in a heady profusion of shapes, fragrances and colours, waiting to be pushed in to floral arrangements here and there. If you're with a date you want to impress, duck in and pluck a long, single stem.

More floral notes drift around the corner at Annick Goutal, an alcove of beauty and charm. The late Goutal was a concert pianist before she turned to perfume making and her unique artisanal fragrances are sold in exquisite, antique-inspired bottles. Goutal's daughter, Camille (who has a fragrance named after her), continues her mother's work. I ask the assistant which scent is her favourite. '*Musc Nomade*,' she answers: a cloud of white musk with amber. I smile when I see *Petite Chérie*, the first perfume of both of my daughters and a lovely gift for a teenage girl. 'Sweet, sassy and mischievous, it's a powdery fragrance with a ripple of peach and pear, and a hint of musk and vanilla.' These sophisticated scents evoke emotion. I sample *Ce Soir Ou Jamais* (tonight or never), before deciding on *Grand Amour*, a sensual fragrance of musk,

Roses at Roses Costes; Annick Goutal perfume

floral and amber, devoted to the powerful force of love.

The romantic mood continues back on Rue Saint-Honoré. Wicked, intoxicating hot chocolate can be had at Jean-Paul Hévin, a renowned chocolate artisan with an upstairs tea salon. The menu of gourmet hot chocolates includes the smooth and silky '4 p.m. aphrodisiac', with fragrant ginger and spices. At the bottom of the courtyard next door is flirty lingerie at Fifi Chachnil, a boudoir of retro froufrou delights with frilly knickers and baby doll négligées in sugar-sweet shades. Further on, next to the cool Colette concept store, is more sugar and spice at Chantal Thomass. The queen of French lingerie created her own brand in the 1960s (bombshell Brigitte Bardot was a fan), and revolutionised the buttoned-up underworld, creating *un frisson* of glamour. These silken dreams are feminine, sensual and seductive, and in a city filled with A and B cups, they go all the way to E. An assistant tells me that Madame Thomass still comes in to help with the window displays.

For a very different taste of the area, Le Rubis is around the corner on Rue du Marché-Saint-Honoré. This rowdy little wine bar appears to have remained unchanged since the 1930s and is a beloved Parisian gathering place for a glass of wine and plate of charcuterie at any time of the day. In fine weather, the crowd spills out to the wine barrels on the footpath. On my last trip to Paris a few months back, I had lunch here with my friend Vince. Fresh from the wide-open spaces of Australia, I felt like a giant tossed into a tiny doll's house, but what a thrilling way to dive right back into Paris's arms! We squeezed up the stairs and into our seats. The little dining room was crowded, noisy and push-and-shove. A bottle of the new season's Beaujolais was plonked on our table and simple plates of home cooking streamed from the minuscule kitchen: *brandade de morue, bœuf bourguignon,* and *jarret de porc* with lentils. It's the kind of basic comfort food you be hard pressed to find in Australia nowadays. In fact, *la grande attraction* here is that the place is so unaffected and unpretentious.

Vince grew up around the corner and has watched the neighbourhood change. 'During the 1950s and 60s, the Marché Saint-Honoré area was all jewellery and furs. In the 1970s and 80s, it was food, and today it is luxury fashion,' he said.

Back on the posh Rue Saint-Honoré, I want to snatch every single piece in the shop at Astier de Villatte. Inspired by old designs and made in the company's Bastille workshop, this cupboard-full of handmade ceramics is simply exquisite. Whimsical jugs, plates and cups woo the shopper in a mix of styles, and overflow with character and charming imperfections. The unique tableware is made from black terracotta clay but glazed to a natural, milky-white finish. There is also a range of irresistible scented candles. Each evokes the scent and ambience of a specific place, from Monte Carlo to the Paris Opera House, and even Rue Saint-Honoré.

Le Rubis

Across the street is Verlet, one of my all-time favourite cafés in Paris, tucked away surprisingly close to the Louvre. This cosy pocket of warmth opened on the street in 1880, and is filled with the welcoming aroma of freshly ground coffee and a band of loyal locals who slip in for a 'lapsang souchong crocodile tea' or *grand pavois* coffee to propel them through the day. There's also a small selection of homemade pastries. The cheery ring of the antique telephone and open sacks of coffee give it a lived-in, comfortable feel, and the counter is constantly cluttered with restaurant orders and bags being prepared for customers to take home. Owner Eric Duchossoy travels the world in search of exotic coffee and rare teas.

Astier de Villatte

A little further on, the Palais Royal is a clandestine parcel of pleasure just steps from the busy Rue de Rivoli. In spring and summer, when the fountains are splashing and the flowers are blooming in the central garden, it is unquestionably one of the most beautiful places in Paris. I take a seat under the clipped lime trees and catch my breath. Locals walk their dogs and read the newspaper. Music wafts from the open windows of apartments above (some of the most sought-after real estate in the city), and restaurant terraces spill on to the garden. Tranquil today, the former royal palace has a colourful history and was once the scene of revolutionary plotting, gambling and debauchery.

Under the stone arcades are specialist shops displaying everything from French military medals and armies of lead soldiers to antique smoking pipes. For a walk through the history of Paris fashion, drop in to the iconic Didier Ludot and rummage through his racks of vintage glam and haute couture from French designers. Across the park is his boutique devoted to the little black dress, La Petite Robe Noire.

Continuing along Rue Saint-Honoré, the mood starts to change and I stumble across La Bague de Kenza, one long party table groaning with Algerian pastries. The colourful store is a feast for the senses and stops me in my tracks. Piled into tottering towers is a rainbow of exotically named delicacies filled with almonds, figs, dates and pistachios, and flavoured with rosewater and honey. Dazzling delights dressed in coats of bright marzipan resemble slices of watermelon, figs, and lemons with green leaves.

Across Rue du Louvre I turn down Rue de l'Arbre-Sec and

into La Galcante. It is possible to become so absorbed in this wonderful, rambling store that an afternoon could soon flick by in a whirl of pleasure. Walls are stacked floor to ceiling with an enormous collection of nicotine-coloured newspapers, vintage *Paris Match* and *Le Petit Journal* magazines. This trove of ancient journals is classified thematically and chronologically, with treasures from fields as varied as sport, politics, cinema and fashion. Box upon box is labelled like a phone book of famous names and once you start lifting those lids, there will be no stopping you. Some of the retro fashion magazine covers are ideal to frame, and make unique souvenirs of Paris. 'The archives date back to 1789, to the French Revolution,' says owner Monsieur Kuzma. 'Birthday newspapers can be sent anywhere in the world.'

I finish my afternoon directly across the road at Le Garde Robe, a lovely little *bar à vin*, all wood and exposed brick, with a glass of *vin naturel* and a plate of ham and cheese. The ever-popular Spring bistro is just around the corner. Afterwards, I might swing by and see if, by some miracle, there has been a cancellation for dinner later tonight. One can only hope. ◊

Palais Royal, La Bague de Kenza pastries, Le Restaurant du Palais Royal, La Galcante

LESCURE >>

A few months ago on a wintry day, I lunched at **Lescure** with my friend Vince. This cosy little spot somehow manages to stay off the radar, despite being close to the Jardin des Tuileries. Passed from father to son since 1919, the restaurant is surprisingly rustic and reasonably priced for such a glamorous part of town. It's like stepping into a tiny country auberge. Copper saucepans, sausages and strings of garlic hang from the rafters. The cuisine is traditional French, with many dishes from the Limousin region. We enjoyed bœuf bourguignon, a plate of cheese and a classic crème caramel.

Restaurant Lescure | 7, Rue de Mondovi, 75001 | ☎ 01 42 60 18 91

ADDRESSES

Annick Goutal
14, Rue de Castiglione, 75001
📞 01 42 60 52 82
www.annickgoutal.com

Astier de Villatte
173, Rue Saint-Honoré, 75001
📞 01 42 60 74 13
www.astierdevillatte.com

La Bague de Kenza
136, Rue Saint-Honoré, 75001
📞 01 42 86 85 23
www.labaguedekenza.com

Bread & Roses
25, Rue Boissy d'Anglas, 75008
📞 01 47 42 40 00
www.breadandroses.fr

Chanel
31, Rue Cambon, 75001
📞 01 44 50 66 00
www.chanel.com

Chantal Thomass
211, Rue Saint-Honoré, 75001
📞 01 42 60 40 56
www.chantalthomass.fr

Didier Ludot
Jardin du Palais Royal, 75001
20–24 Galerie de Montpensier
📞 01 42 96 06 56
www.didierludot.fr

Fauchon
24-26-30, Place de la Madeleine, 75008
📞 01 70 39 38 00
www.fauchon.com

Fifi Chachnil
231, Rue Saint-Honoré, 75001
📞 01 42 61 21 83
www.fifichachnil.com

La Galcante
52, Rue de l'Arbre-Sec, 750010
📞 01 44 77 8744
www.lagalcante.com

La Garde Robe
41, Rue de l'Arbre-Sec, 75001
📞 01 49 26 90 60

Hôtel Costes
239, Rue Saint-Honoré, 75001
📞 01 42 44 50 00

Hédiard
21, Place de la Madeleine, 75008
📞 01 43 12 88 88
www.hediard.fr

Jean-Paul Hévin
231, Rue Saint-Honoré, 75001
📞 01 55 35 35 96
www.jphevin.com

Ladurée
16, Rue Royale, 75008
📞 01 42 60 21 79
www.laduree.fr

ADDRESSES

Mandarin Oriental, Paris

251, Rue Saint-Honoré, 75001
☎ 01 70 98 78 88
www.mandarinoriental.com

Musée Maxim's

3, Rue Royale, 75008
☎ 01 42 65 30 47
www.maxims-musee-artnouveau.
com

La Petite Robe Noire

125, Galerie de Valois
☎ 01 40 15 01 04

Pierre Hermé

4, Rue Cambon, 75001
☎ 01 58 62 43 17
www.pierreherme.com

Roses Costes Dani Roses

☎ 01 4244 5009
www.hotelcostes.com

Le Rubis

10, Rue du Marché Saint-
Honoré, 75001
☎ 01 42 61 03 34

Verlet

256, Rue Saint-Honoré, 75001
☎ 01 42 60 67 39
www.cafesverlet.com

CHAPTER THREE

Strawberry Tarts & Vanilla
ICE CREAM

◆◆◆

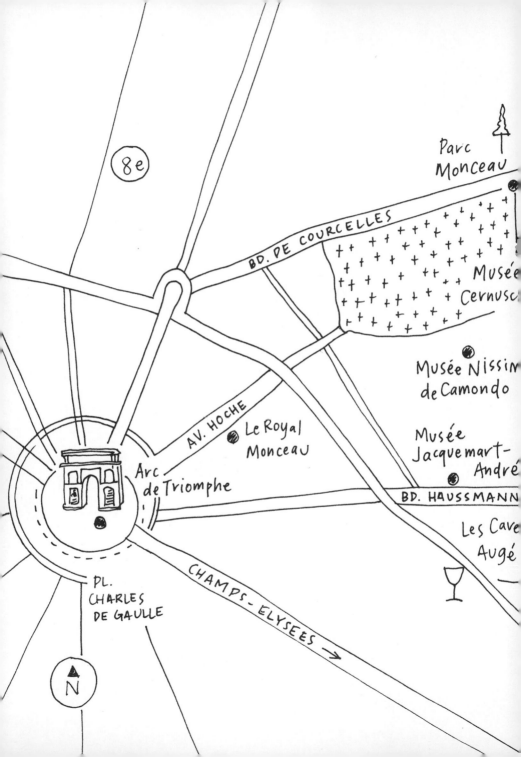

There are dozens of intriguing small museums sprinkled throughout Paris and just as I cross one off my mushrooming list, I discover another – like the new chocolate museum, **Le Musée Gourmand du Chocolat**; or **Fondation Henri Cartier-Bresson**, devoted to the famous photographer who co-founded Magnum Photos. Even if you reside in Paris you can't quite ever get a lid on them all. Friends lived in the same building as **Le Musée Clemenceau** but we still never managed to get there. (The tiny apartment is left exactly as it was the day the French statesman, physician and writer died in 1929.) Nor did we make it to the **Edith Piaf Museum**. Far off the beaten boulevard, a visit requires a phone call to the curator to arrange.

In Paris, it seems, just as there will always be another Berthillon ice cream flavour to try, there will always be another cosy museum to visit. Many are set in the original homes of artists, writers and collectors, giving an entrée into their private worlds as well as providing a venue to view their works or idiosyncratic collections. They offer a rush of privilege and a warmth and intimacy impossible to find in vast galleries, and personally, I find them far more rewarding. Each time I climb, with anticipation, up a flight of stone steps, or pass through an elaborate cloistered doorway, I feel like an honoured guest invited to a private party.

These appetising little gems offer a refreshing taste of the different flavours of Paris, and a welcome antidote to long lines at the Louvre. Their manageable size means they can be enjoyed in the space of an hour or so, creating a delightful diversion in a day of shopping, sightseeing or eating. One is instantly connected with the history and culture of Paris, but before the scoop falls from the cone you are back outside.

These lesser-known addresses are often found in the most unexpected of places – perhaps at the end of a cobbled lane, or in a nondescript apartment building with no more in the way of announcement than a small brass plaque and a French flag flapping overhead. Others, like the Musée Nissim de Camondo, hide in historic mansions.

Before a visit to this secluded museum on a cool spring day, I meet my friend Jocelyn for a light lunch in the Grand Salon of Le Royal Monceau. It's a casual yet elegant spot with all-day dining and divine pastries by Pierre Hermé (see page 25). Opened in 1928, this luxury boutique hotel with a fabulous spa was taken over by Raffles in 2008, and after an extensive two-year renovation, is once again up there with the best. It earned its first Michelin stars in 2013: one for its French restaurant, La Cuisine, and the other for Il Carpaccio, making it the only Michelin-starred Italian restaurant in Paris. Modern and sophisticated, the prestigious hotel is just a short walk from both the Champs-Elysées and the elegant Parc Monceau, one of the city's loveliest gardens.

It is here on the edge of the park that the Musée Nissim de Camondo is nestled, cloaked in greenery. I confess it's a treasure that took me years to discover, despite Parc Monceau being our family's adopted backyard. Although the museum overlooks the gardens, the entrance and signage are on Rue Monceau, and I mistook it for merely another *hôtel particulier* (grand townhouse) on the park. Even many Parisians aren't familiar with it so it's unlikely to be crowded. I think it's one of the most underrated museums in the city.

> 'Age does not diminish the extreme disappointment of having a scoop of ice cream fall from the cone.'
>
> JIM FIEBIG

Count Moïse de Camondo, a renowned Parisian banker who hailed from a powerful Sephardic Jewish banking family, inherited his parents' property on the park in 1910. Already a great collector of eighteenth-century furniture and decorative arts, he demolished the house and built a glittering mansion, inspired by the Petit Trianon at Versailles, to house his collection.

Musée Nissim de Camondo

The wealthy banker lived here in style, adding to his remarkable collection over the years. On his death in 1935, Moïse de Camondo bequeathed his mansion and its extraordinary contents to Les Arts Décoratifs, requesting that the museum be named in memory of his only son, Nissim, who was killed in combat during World War I. He also stipulated that the furniture and objects be kept in their original positions. Moïse did not live to see the further tragedy in store for his family; during World War II Moïse's only daughter Béatrice, his son-in-law and two grandchildren perished at Auschwitz. Frozen in time, the museum offers a fascinating portal into an aristocratic family shadowed by a sad story, and a wonderful glimpse into the decorative arts of the eighteenth century.

As I follow the audio tour (which takes me a mere fifty minutes), there are many quiet corners in which to contemplate the house in its halcyon days. Room after room is filled with palatial furniture, paintings, clocks and *objets d'art*. Amongst the many treasures: vases that once adorned the private apartments of Queen Marie-Antoinette at Versailles, a carpet from the Savonnerie manufactory supplied in 1678 for the Grande

Galerie in the Louvre, Aubusson tapestries illustrating La Fontaine's Fables, and pieces of silverware gleaned from a service commissioned by Catherine the Great of Russia. I love the dining room looking on to the garden with the table set beautifully for dinner. It's hard to resist taking a seat. Next door is a small porcelain room built especially to display pieces from two Sèvres dinner services, considered the finest of the French porcelains. Peering through the French doors of the Great Drawing Room that lead to the garden, I view Parc Monceau through the trees from an entirely different perspective.

Parc Monceau

The Monceau quarter, on the cupid's bow of the 8th arrondissement, became newly fashionable in the nineteenth century, and this surprising museum perfectly captures the extravagance and opulence of the area at that time. So too do the nearby Musée Cernuschi, with its impressive displays of Chinese art and exotic Far East treasures, and the Musée Jacquemart-André, both of which are also housed in elegant *hôtels particuliers.*

For me, the centrepiece and warm heart of the quarter will always be Parc Monceau, a gentle place filled with fond memories. I take a stroll after my visit to Musée Nissim de Camondo and as I enter through the familiar gilded gates, I once again bump into classic, old-fashioned Paris. Au pairs push prams along the gravel pathways, the same paths that we crunched over a thousand times on the way to and from school. Spotless little cherubs with bobs and bows still play in the playground and ride the carousel. The green benches are dotted with people reading and munching on baguette sandwiches, and there are far more joggers than I remember. Another change is that you can now sit on the grass. No longer is it *interdit*! The lawns don't look as perfectly clipped as they used to, but you can't have it both ways.

Parc Monceau was created by the Duc de Chartres and the original gardens were known as the Folie de Chartres. Various architectural follies still remain, and lend a kind of romantic melancholy to the English-style grounds. A lap will reveal a miniature pyramid, a Chinese fort and a moss-covered Corinthian colonnade that runs around the edge of a lily pond. Scattered throughout the park, amongst the rose gardens and greenery, are six Belle Epoque statues of great French writers and musicians. It was also the site of the first parachute landing in 1797. Be sure to take a photo through the park's ornate grille on Avenue Van-Dyck back towards the Arc de Triomphe.

I exit Parc Monceau here and walk south on Rue de Courcelles towards the Musée Jacquemart-André on Boulevard Haussmann. Back in the late nineteenth century, the boulevard was up-and-coming, a newly fashionable address lined with lavish townhouses where gossip often centred on which pretty *jeune fille* would snaffle Edouard André, one of Paris's most eligible bachelors who lived in a mansion on the boulevard. Society went into shock when the fabulously wealthy Protestant banker and art collector chose the plain Catholic spinster and portrait painter, Mademoiselle Nélie Jacquemart, aged nearly forty!

Edouard and Nélie's happy union, however, was all about a shared passion for art: they amassed the finest private art collection in Paris and dedicated their lives to acquiring masterpieces. The couple travelled for months every year, mostly to Italy, where they scoured the cities for works from the Renaissance period, attending auctions to snap up world-class paintings, sculptures, tapestries and giant murals. Their insatiable artistic

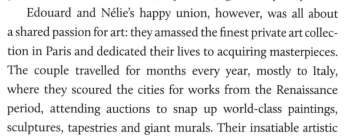

curiosity also led them to accumulate an arresting ensemble of smaller *objets d'art,* from Indian furniture to Persian antiquities. Under the guidance of the most prominent museum curators of the time, their vast collection continued to grow. On Nélie's death in 1912 the mansion and extraordinary collection of art was donated to l'Institut de France for us all to enjoy. In fact, the Parisians themselves are loyal and devoted patrons of this pearl off the tourist track. On weekends, it can get quite crowded.

I step from the carriage driveway and, feeling like Cinderella, ascend the stone steps, which are guarded by two sculptured lions. Modern Paris fades and I am swept back to La Belle Epoque. It is partly the splendour of the mansion itself that draws me back to this self-contained world of art and beauty time and again, for this must-see museum manages to retain the intimacy of a private home despite being awash with grand art. Room by room the couple's extraordinary life unfolds. I drift from the glass-roofed Winter Garden, a sunny oasis of greenery and gleaming marble, to the Music Room, where privileged guests once gathered for classical concerts. With the aid of the audio guide, a (candle) light is thrown on the glitzy lifestyle of the haute bourgeoisie. Once the setting for many a society reception, it's fun to envisage the candlelit parties, attended by the elite of Paris to the strains of live chamber music. I can almost hear the swishing silk.

The residence also features French, Dutch and English masters. There are works by Fragonard, Boucher and Chardin.

Footpath
near Musée
Jacquemart-André

Rembrandts and Van Dycks hang in the library, a Gainsborough in the smoking room. Up the gorgeous double staircase, the pair even kept their very own 'Italian Museum'. Crammed with fifteenth-century sculptures, Botticellis and Mantegnas, the magnificent collection was reserved as a delightful after-dinner treat for their guests and connoisseurs of the art world. Who could fail to be impressed by Uccello's *Saint George and the Dragon*?

However, there is another reason why this sublime townhouse with its dazzling collection of art will always stay on my list of favourite museums. Housed in the Andrés' former dining room is one of the most beautiful tea salons in Paris, slung with Belgian tapestries and crowned with a beguiling ceiling mural by Tiepolo. Sightseeing can be hard work, and there is nothing like a good tea room to provide a delightful refuge and a reviving pause. On summer days, you can also sip tea or eat lunch on the terrace. Adored by the locals, the tea room can also become quite crowded, especially when the popular weekend brunch is served. It can be accessed independently but does not take reservations.

Under Tiepolo's fresco, I pour tea perfumed with red fruits from my monogrammed teapot and order a pastry from the dessert cart. Next to me on the slender gilt wood chairs are two well-dressed children with their grandmother, hoeing into vanilla ice cream and discussing their favourite paintings. What a wonderful outing they'll have to remember! Amongst the delights on today's trolley is a wickedly dark chocolate tart, a pistachio macaron cake filled with mousseline cream and fresh raspberries, and a glistening *tarte aux fraises* (strawberry tart). The small selection of *pâtisseries* is sourced from Stohrer, the oldest pastry shop in Paris, where the ceilings and walls are exquisitely painted with garlands of flowers and murals of women bearing wheat sheaves and pastries. A fitting match. Nicholas Stohrer was a pastry chef to King Louis XV at the court of Versailles before opening his own shop on the Rue Montorgueil market street in 1730. Just as it did back then, specialities include one of the classics of French pastry, *baba au rhum,* a little yeast cake liberally doused with rum, and *puits d'amour,* caramelised wells of love filled with vanilla pastry cream. It's worth a detour.

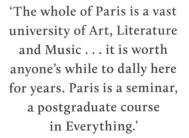

> 'The whole of Paris is a vast university of Art, Literature and Music . . . it is worth anyone's while to dally here for years. Paris is a seminar, a postgraduate course in Everything.'
>
> JAMES THURBER

And so with dinner a long way off (most locals dine no earlier than 8.30 p.m.), I tuck politely into my strawberry tart, aware that I am being watched from above by Venetian nobles who lean comically over the painted balustrade. A cheeky little monkey hangs its tail daringly over the fresco's edge. Afterwards, I shall slip into Les Caves Augé, one of the city's most historic and beautiful wine shops, just as Marcel Proust used to. A serious wine store crammed with precious bottles, owner Marc Sibard offers thousands of French and foreign selections from small producers (*s'il vous plaît,* don't even think about pulling those bottles down for yourself!). The calendar for the popular free pavement tastings with regional winemakers is available on the website and dates are worth noting. But for now I shall relax in this fine Parisian jewel and relish the ritual of taking tea – French style. ◊

ADDRESSES

Les Caves Augé
116, Boulevard Haussmann, 75008
☎ 01 45 22 16 97
www.cavesauge.com

Musée Cernuschi
7, Avenue Vélasquez, 75008
☎ 01 53 96 21 50
www.cernuschi.paris.fr

Musée Jacquemart-André
158, Boulevard Haussmann, 75008
☎ 01 45 62 11 59
www.musee-jacquemart-andre.com
The café is open daily from 11.45 a.m. to 5.30 p.m. (lunch from 11.45 a.m. to 3 p.m. and tea from 3 p.m. to 5.30 p.m.). The popular brunch is served Saturday and Sunday from 11 a.m. to 3 p.m.

Musée Nissim de Camondo
63, Rue Monceau, 75008
☎ 01 53 89 06 50
www.lesartsdecoratifs.fr

Le Royal Monceau – Raffles Paris
37, Avenue Hoche, 75008
☎ 01 42 99 88 00
www.leroyalmonceau.com

Stohrer
51, Rue Montorgueil, 75002
☎ 01 42 33 38 20
www.stohrer.fr

CHAPTER FOUR

Mousse au CHOCOLAT

♦♦♦

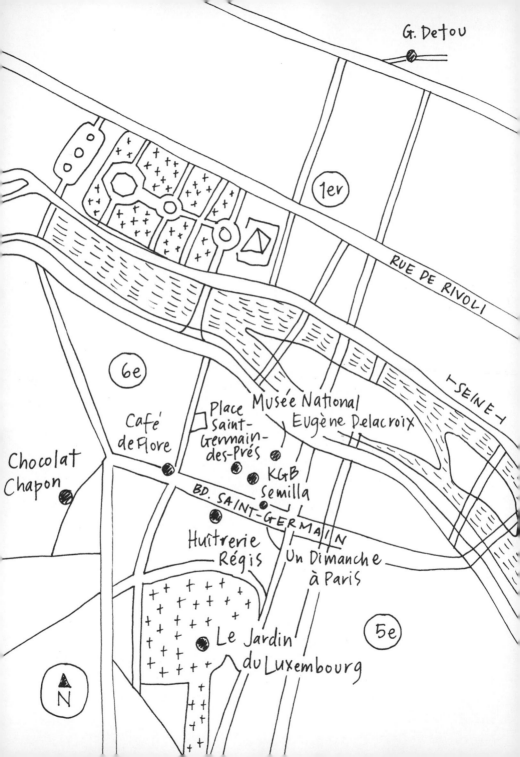

It's just before ten in the morning when I arrive at Place Saint-Germain-des-Prés in the heart of the Left Bank. The ancient square is bathed in a soft morning light and deserted except for a few pecking pigeons. As I cross the cobbles, I hear chinking crockery and the murmur of voices on the terrace of the famous literary café, Les Deux Magots. Waiters in long aprons dash about under the legendary green awnings with trays of pastries and coffee. Under the bell tower of the Eglise de Saint-Germain-des-Prés, the oldest surviving abbey church in Paris, I wait with anticipation. This is the meeting point for my **Chocolate Walk** with Context Travel.

The acclaimed tour company has revolutionised day tours in cities across the world from New York to Shanghai with their small-group 'walking seminars'. Aimed at the 'intellectually curious traveller', they are led by a network of English-speaking specialists in their fields (called docents), from art historians to gastronomes and architects who connect guests to their city as a local friend would. In addition to tours such as Notre Dame & Gothic Paris, and the Louvre Crash Course, Context runs a number of food-focused walks and classes in Paris. A mosey around a market with a culinary expert is one option, or perhaps you would prefer to whip up a few miniature versions of classic French desserts. This cooking class – Café Gourmand: A Parisian Dessert Trend – explores the fashion of coffee accompanied by several mini desserts.

However, the word 'chocolate' is powerful, and the idea of a delicious jaunt through the Left Bank seeking out some of the best on offer, in all its luxurious forms, is difficult to top. After all,

Paris is home to some of the world's best chocolatiers and *pâtis-siers*, each with their own specialities, and the heart of the Left Bank has a frighteningly high concentration of upscale stores. The Chocolate Walk is led by one of Context's professional gastronomes, who through extensive research and personal experience (ie tasting), have sought out their favourite places to indulge. Guests learn about the rich dessert history associated with Paris, the magical secrets of chocolate making, and sample a few goodies along the way.

Our docent breezes across the square and greets our group warmly. Tours are limited to six people, but the only other partici-pants today are a mother and daughter visiting from the States, so I feel rather spoilt. We walk up Boulevard Saint-Germain past Les Deux Magots and the celebrated Café de Flore. 'You'll find mostly tourists at Les Deux Magots, but locals go to Flore,' says our docent. 'It's the ultimate people-watching spot.'

Our first stop is Debauve & Gallais, the oldest chocolate store in Paris. Opposite the Université Paris Descartes' Faculty of Medicine, it was opened as a pharmacy in 1800, prescribing full-flavoured chocolate rich in cocoa, which was lauded for its health benefits. The bewitching store feels like an old-fashioned chemist and is the work of Percier and Fontaine, the architects commis-sioned by Napoleon for Josephine's country residence, Château de Malmaison. Debauve was formerly the appointed chocolate maker and pharmacist to the royal family, and the stylish boxes are still sealed with the King of France's coat of arms. Brillat-Savarin, Proust and Balzac were also fans of their chocolate.

The smell of chocolate is hypnotising. Soft caramels, truffles, and single-origin chocolate ganaches are meticulously displayed like jewels around the half-moon-shaped counter. Boxes of *incroyables* beckon. A favourite of Van Gogh's, these hulls of nougatine are flooded with bittersweet dark chocolate ganache.

Then there are the famous *pistoles de Marie-Antoinette,* wafer-thin coins of snappy chocolate made with varying percentages of cocoa, originally created to help the queen take her bitter-tasting medicine. Our docent gathers a stash of her favourites and we step into the quiet courtyard next door. As we taste, we are given a quick lesson in how chocolate is made, tasting a pure chocolate bean against chocolate samples with varying percentages of cocoa.

Every store we will visit today buys its chocolate from Valrhona. This French chocolate manufacturer near Lyon focuses on high-grade, luxury chocolate. If you love baking, I recommend whizzing over to G. Detou, a fabulous wholesale grocery store on the Right Bank specialising in baking supplies, where you can pick up Valrhona bars at very attractive prices. Snaffle a bag of Valrhona Cocoa Powder to take home if you have room. Dark, rich and full of flavour, there is nothing like it. As well as giant boxes of vanilla pods and candied violets there's a well-stocked pantry of regional and unusual products: great foodie gifts that are light on the purse.

> '1 was unable to lift my mouth from the delicious edge of its cup. Chocolate to die for, thick, velvety, fragrant, exhilarating.'
>
> GUY DE MAUPASSANT,
> French author (1850–1893)

As we continue walking, we pass women dressed in chic black. 'You will always be in vogue in Paris if you wear black,' our docent smiles. My theory is that with chocolates and pastries around every corner you'd be mad *not* to dress in black. It is so forgiving.

Our appetites are whetted for the next rendezvous. We learn that Patrice Chapon has only been in chocolate seriously for a decade or so. Before that, he was the official ice cream maker to Buckingham Palace, and he still makes ice cream, including a wicked salted-butter caramel flavour. We also discover he operates a Chocolate Mousse Bar, with several different flavours on offer. 'He has won first prize, twice, for the best chocolate in the city, and has entered the best creation at the Salon du Chocolat,' says our docent.

An irresistible annual event in October, the Salon du Chocolat is the place to discover new artisans, products and trends in chocolate. There are demonstrations, exhibits and a bookshop filled with chocolate-related titles. Every year there is a fashion show. Chocolatiers pair up with designers and parade clothes made out of chocolate. This year the theme was lingerie. The public can taste chocolate from all over France and the world, but keep in mind that while there is an entrance fee, there are surprisingly few free samples.

Once inside Chocolat Chapon, I am rapidly under the spell of chocolate. A place that exudes pleasure and conjures dreams, it oozes with warmth and emotion. Chapon writes on his website that he 'remains faithful to the child within' and that 'A bar of chocolate embodies a dream transporting one's desires, and a piece of the bar is a fragment of this dream. My aim with that chocolate bar is more to feed the childhood memories rather than the appetites.'

How can one not be enchanted!

The tiny, old-world shop was once an ancient horse-butcher's. Meat hooks still hang on the façade. Inside, enormous copper cauldrons act as lampshades and the back walls are covered with vintage chocolate moulds, adding charm and sparkle. In an old-fashioned ice chest, tubs of light and airy sorbet explode with fruit flavours. Bars of single-origin chocolate beckon and the counter is covered with handmade chocolates. We taste Chapon's *praline baies roses* (praline with pink cherries), which won first prize at the Salon du Chocolate 2007 and his *dome praline fondant au sel de Guérande* (almond, hazelnut and pistachio praline with

Chocolat Chapon

Guérande salt), a delicious indulgence that won the coveted Grand Prix du Chocolat from the City of Paris.

Despite the magnificence of these chocolates, it is the luscious *bar à mousse* that draws us in. Several flavours are available, made with quality chocolate from different corners of the globe. The bar is only open during the autumn and winter months, for everything in France has a season. We opt for 'Cuba', which has a smoky, woody taste and is fresh in the mouth. We're warned that the mousse is extremely rich, so we decide to share a cornet and watch in wonder as the enormous satiny concoction is scooped into a paper cone and topped with praline. Our docent produces four tiny spoons and we dig in. We never do quite reach the bottom.

We make our way past a poetic florist shop where heavily scented hyacinths and Christmas trees take over the footpath. Our next stop is a modern *pâtisserie* and *chocolaterie,* thickly robed in dark chocolate with bursts of colour and light. My first impression is of a state-of-the-art jewellery shop. Macarons are stacked in giant test tubes of varying heights, each containing a different colour and flavour. Built into the walls are glass-fronted showcases presenting pastries in the spotlight, created by the 2003 French Champion of Desserts. Our docent orders a vanilla *mille-feuille* to taste and a fresh one is assembled 'on the spot'. As we leave, I notice the giant, soft pillows of marsh-mallow: *les guimauves*. They seem to be everywhere at the moment. Here, they do them in vanilla, lemon and *combava* (the fruit of the kaffir lime), but some pastry makers are flavouring them with bourbon or fruit. Cassis is also popular.

We stop at a tranquil little park to taste our pastry. The test is if it's crisp on top. There is nothing worse than a soggy *mille-feuille*! As our docent cuts through the layers of crisp pastry, she explains that quite a few of the best pâtisseries in town are now making them to order, on the spot. 'It's a new trend called *mille-feuille à la minute*. That way you are guaranteed freshness.' A classic *mille-feuille* has three layers of puff pastry and two layers of vanilla cream. Ours has creamy Tahitian vanilla, which is ever so soft and yielding against the perky layers of flaky pastry.

Today is Thanksgiving in the United States, and as we enter our final shop, my new American friends are delighted to find a huge orange pumpkin taking centre stage on a platform with its own light show. This *chocolatier* is renowned for his chocolate sculptures. Last Easter there was a chicken and a gigantic nest of real eggs, each painstakingly emptied and filled with praline. Along one wall are platters of caramels, some infused with peach and blackcurrant. The chocolate counter is a mosaic of multi-coloured squares. We pick out a few samples to take away. These are extravagant chocolates with intoxicating scents and flavours. I choose one filled with an eruption of tropical vanilla and another with pepper and mint. Pepper with chocolate is a big trend, as is salt or tonka beans. The assistant pops a luminous green marble of caramel sharpened with lime in my bag, and lastly, a ganache with essence of basil and a closing burst of lemon. With a mouth full of chocolate, I say my goodbyes and walk merrily on my way.

> 'If you are not feeling well, if you have not slept, chocolate will revive you. But you have no chocolate! I think of that again and again! My dear, how will you ever manage?'
>
> MARQUISE DE SÉVIGNÉ
> (French author and lady of fashion)
> February 11, 1677

◇◇◇◇◇

A little giddy from all the sweet morsels, I'm already plotting lunch. Choosing a good neighbourhood bistro, however, can be as difficult as picking from a box of chocolates. Each has its own merit, distinctive flavour and character, and what appeals to one may not tempt another. I flick through the little black book in my head and open it to Saint-Germain-de-Prés. Huîtrerie Régis – what's better than a dozen pristine oysters with Kayser bread, good butter and a glass of Sancerre? This simple little oyster bar with just a snatch of tables serves some of the best in Paris. Or there's KGB (Kitchen Galerie Bis), the colourful annex of William Ledeuil's popular one-Michelin-star restaurant Ze Kitchen Galerie on the same street. The chef is renowned for his inventive and modern Franco-Asian cuisine, and his bistro version is just as delicious.

Here in the heart of Saint-Germain-de-Prés, camera-toting crowds and a new chic breed of Left Bankers now sit where Jean-Paul Sartre and Simone de Beauvoir used to scribble fervently. Luxurious fashion houses from across the river have packed their designer bags and moved in along the grand boulevards. Some of the most expensive real estate in the city is here, and it's worth noting that it's more difficult than one imagines finding a good-value lunch, and at popular addresses, it's best to book in advance.

I meander on towards the river, dodging the queue outside Pierre Hermé's sleek pastry shop on Rue Bonaparte and passing the tranquil Place Saint-Sulpice. It's a lovely spot to sit in spring and summer, with a restful central fountain and pink flowering chestnut trees. I continue, turning left down Rue de Seine where I swipe a seat at Semilla, the latest venture of American Juan Sanchez and New Zealander Drew Harré. Lunch problem solved! The successful duo is also behind the dependable restaurant and wine bar, Fish La Boissonnerie, which has recently undergone a major renovation, and Cosi sandwich shop on this same little strip.

The newly renovated space at Semilla has exposed stone walls, overhead beams and an open kitchen run by Eric Trochon and his dynamic team of young chefs from the Ecole Ferrandi. Semilla offers what many visitors want to find on a bistro menu but often don't – a vegetarian option, dishes available in small servings, high-quality ingredients from some of the country's best producers, and a mix of French classics and inventive, cosmopolitan dishes. The short, thoughtful menu is also reasonably priced for this neck of the woods. In fact, Semilla offers the whole box of chocolates. The *carte de vins* presents well-chosen selections by the glass, carafe and bottle. Sanchez also runs the beloved wine store La Dernière Goutte around the corner. He personally handpicks estate-bottled wines from small growers, mostly organic,

and conducts free tastings with visiting producers.

After lunch I head off into the surrounding maze of small streets chockfull of antique shops, art galleries and one-off boutiques to arrive at a favourite spot in the quarter, the intimate Place de Furstenberg. Encircled by a hectic, modern Paris, this tiny square manages to stay unruffled, like an elegant, older woman unfazed by the passing of time. The square's charm lies in the central antique candelabrum, which is guarded by a ring of Empress trees. Especially in the evenings when the soft glow of the street lamp throws shadows across the street, it is surely one of the most romantic little spots in Paris. The evocative square was featured in Vincente Minnelli's film *Gigi*

Place de
Furstenberg

and has been painted by many artists. The Romantic painter Eugène Delacroix lived on the edge of the square and loved it most in the early morning light.

Behind a set of heavy green doors, you can still visit the painter's last home, now the Musée Delacroix. I slip in for a quick look at the lovely garden studio and first-floor apartment filled with works of art, personal memorabilia and keepsakes. Delacroix moved here in 1857 in order to finish three striking murals in the nearby Church of Saint-Sulpice. You can still marvel at them today in the church's Chapel of the Holy Angels.

In and around Rue de Furstenberg is a swathe of fabric houses as well as design and home decoration stores. I find sumptuous windows dressed with yards of billowing fabric and pretty curtain tassels. There are tinkling chandeliers and beautiful bed linen in shades of vanilla, cinnamon and oyster-shell grey. It's the quarter to screech to a stop at when you're ready to decorate that little *pied-à-terre* you dream about having in Paris one day.

I'm dragging my feet, so it's time for a rest and afternoon tea, and it's only fitting that I end my day soothed by chocolate. I head towards Cour du Commerce Saint André and its adjoining scramble of courtyards. Easy to miss, this secret passageway running between Boulevard Saint-Germain and Rue Saint André des Arts instantly tosses you into the magical world of old Paris. You'll find the back entrance of Le Procope (the oldest existing café in Paris, dating to 1686), a popular haunt among intellectuals, where Voltaire was known to throw back forty cups of coffee a day and Napoleon's hat is still on display. It was where Dr Guillotin fine-tuned his 'philanthropic decapitating machine' on sheep, and Marat ran off his revolutionary paper, *L'Ami du Peuple*. Nowadays, the scene is more tranquil.

I navigate the rough cobblestones, peeking through open doorways and wrought-iron gates into quiet, private courtyards, before stepping across the threshold into Un Dimanche à Paris.

It doesn't take long to realise that this elegant temple to chocolate is an essential destination for chocoholics, one that will leave your heart pounding. Under one roof you can purchase, sip, savour, learn about and cook with chocolate, as well as watch it being made. Downstairs, dreamy pastries pose in the boutique and you can peer through into the chocolate workshop to see the talented pastry chefs in action. There is also a contemporary restaurant and *salon du chocolat* where chocolate is utilised in many of the creations. Patrons can choose their own pastry from the boutique, and there are desserts 'made to order'. 'We are well known for our *soufflé au chocolat*,' says chocolate expert Pierre Cluizel, the imaginative man from the renowned French chocolate family who created the concept. Cluizel has recently opened a new 'gastronomic restaurant' upstairs. I don't think the man ever stops; maybe it's something to do with all that *chocolat*.

Un Dimanche
à Paris

Here in his universe of chocolate, cutting-edge excellence and creativity collide with French history and tradition. Prominently incorporated into the interior design of the complex is a beautiful, restored section of the thirteenth-century *Tour Philippe Auguste*, a vestige of the oldest known city wall. Upstairs, in addition to the restaurant, is a hands-on cooking school devoted to, *oui*, all things chocolate. Translation can be arranged for groups. In the evening, the chocolate lounge opens, where you can relax with a chocolate-inspired cocktail mixed to meet your individual desires. Sunday brunch is also very popular, which brings me to the store's name – A Sunday in Paris. Sundays are associated with good times spent with those you love, with relaxation, pleasure . . . and chocolate.

Now, as hot chocolate is the speciality of the house, how could I refuse? The perfect way to finish a day dipped in chocolate. It arrives in a porcelain pitcher with a little wooden handle and a wooden stirrer moored inside. How, also, could I possibly refuse a decadent *gourmandise* selection, a dessert plate with a line-up of four mini delights?

In need of a recovery stroll, I head towards the beautiful Luxembourg Gardens via Rue de Seine. The city's largest park, edged by Montparnasse, Saint-Germain-des-Prés and the Latin Quarter, is an integral part of the Left Bank.

Anyone who knows the top end of Rue de Seine also knows that it is humanly impossible to pass by Gérard Mulot without stopping to ogle the dazzling, multi-coloured cakes and pastries in the window. Mulot makes magnificent fruit tarts; his square strawberry tart was ranked number one in the city by *Figaroscope* magazine in 2011 and he is a perennial contender for the best macaron in Paris. Today in the window of his *belle pâtisserie* I spy his fabulous Amaryllis, a family-sized macaron sprinkled with dried fruit, enclosing vanilla cream and decorated with fresh raspberries, and his equally fabulous Macaronade, a base of pistachio macaron with *crème pistache* and marmalade raspberries perfumed with violets.

Un Dimanche
à Paris

I find a chair in the gardens by the main fountain and lounge in a pool of late afternoon sun. I won't need dinner tonight, but on the off-chance I'm peckish, I have a few chocolates to polish off. ◊

PARIS WALKS >>

The budget-friendly tour company **Paris Walks** also offers a Chocolate Tour several times a month, a trail of dark chocolate that takes you to a variety of superb chocolatiers on the Right Bank. Each entertaining session consists of an alluring mix of historical gossip, chocolate appreciation and samples. Tours are in English and the company offers an assortment of engaging walks ranging from The Medieval Latin Quarter to The Opera House, led by a small team of professional guides who know Paris well. Adding to the appeal is that most tours do not require reservations – just show up at the meeting point, rain or shine.

Paris Walks | ☎ 01 48 09 21 40 | www.paris-walks.com

ADDRESSES

Café de Flore
172, Boulevard Saint-Germain, 75006
📞 01 45 48 55 26
www.cafedeflore.fr

Chocolat Chapon
69, Rue du Bac, 75007
📞 01 42 22 95 98
www.chocolat-chapon.com

Context Travel
www.contexttravel.com

Debauve & Gallais
30, Rue des Saints-Pères, 75007
📞 01 45 48 54 67
www.debauve-et-gallais.com

La Dernière Goutte
6, Rue Bourbon le Château, 75006
📞 01 43 29 11 62
www.laderniEregoutte.net

Un Dimanche à Paris
4-6-8 Cour du Commerce Saint André, 75006
📞 01 56 81 18 18
www.un-dimanche-a-paris.com

G. Detou
58, Rue Tiquetonne, 75002
📞 01 42 36 54 67
www.gdetou.com

Gérard Mulot
76, Rue de Seine, 75006
📞 01 43 26 85 77
www.gerard-mulot.com

Huîtrerie Régis
3, Rue Montfaucon, 75006
📞 01 44 41 10 07
www.huitrerieregis.com

KGB
(Kitchen Galerie Bis)
25, Rue des Grands Augustins, 75006
📞 01 46 33 00 85
www.zekitchengalerie.fr

Musée National Eugène Delacroix
6, Rue Furstenberg, 75006
📞 01 44 41 86 50
www.musee-delacroix.fr

Salon du Chocolat
Venue: Viparis Porte de Versailles
www.salonduchocolat.fr

Semilla
54, Rue de Seine, 75006
📞 01 43 54 34 50

CHAPTER FIVE

Camembert de Normandie & a DEMI-BAGUETTE

◆◆◆

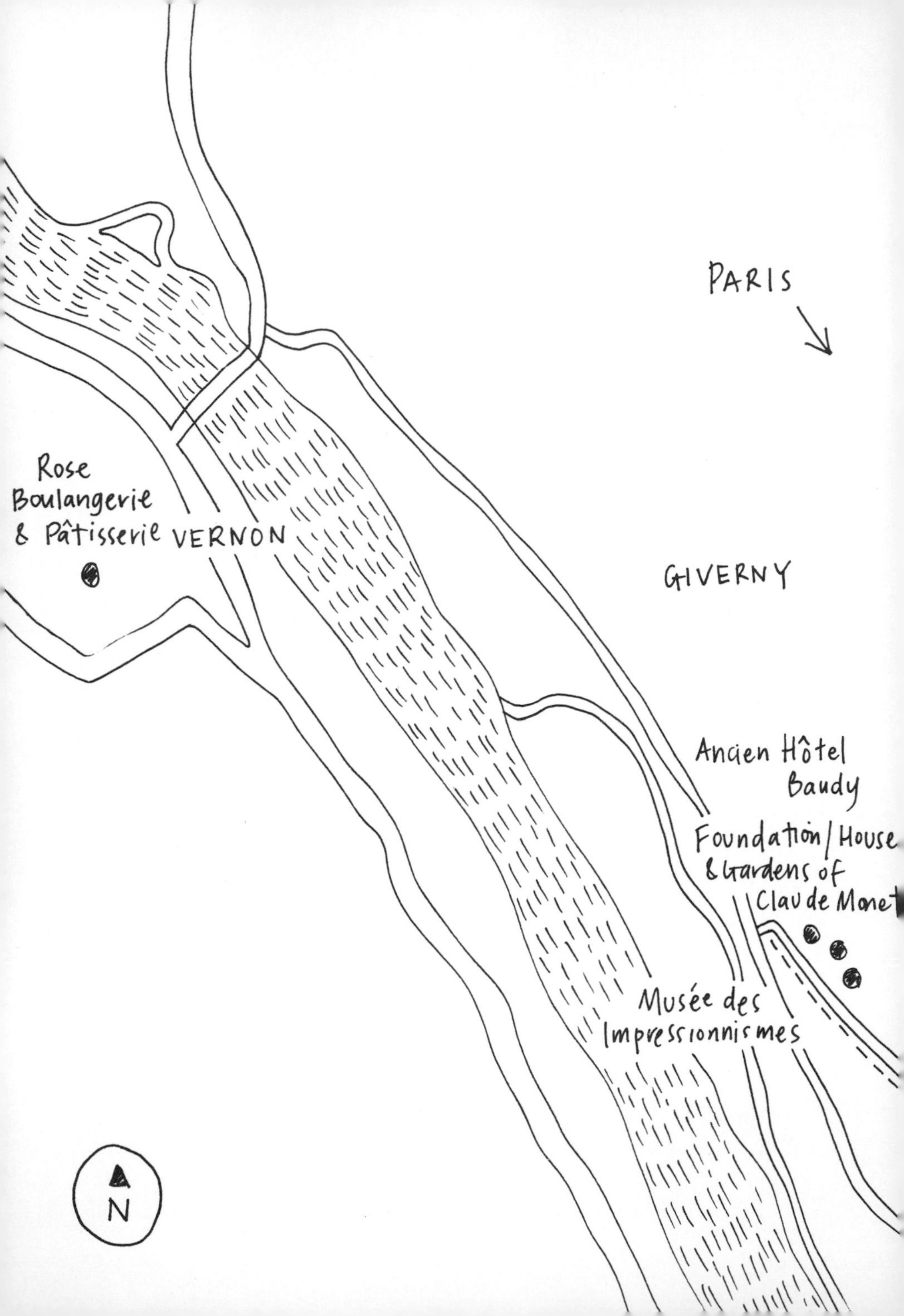

PARIS

Rose
Boulangerie
& Pâtisserie VERNON

GIVERNY

Ancien Hôtel
Baudy

Foundation/House
& Gardens of
Claude Monet

Musée des
Impressionnismes

N

Our train bound for Normandy pulls out of the station and slowly gathers speed. Soon, we are flashing past sleepy villages, sunflowers and fields of waving corn. It's strange to think that the Impressionist painter Claude Monet took this very same journey from Gare Saint-Lazare to his country house in Giverny many times. In fact, our excursion today with **Fat Tire Bike Tours** is a kind of Monet timeline – born in Paris in 1840, he spent his later life in Giverny and today we are following in his footsteps. The Father of Impressionism even painted the Saint-Lazare train station several times in 1877, capturing its billowing clouds of steam. Indeed, this subject was an ideal setting for a man intent on grasping things that were transient – and he loved water in all its forms. Paris was changing rapidly too and Monet wanted to paint subjects that were real, and happening in his time.

Kit, the guide for our group today, is a passionate American with a background in fine art and art history, and our leisurely train ride proves to be an intriguing, moving lecture.

Designed for the English-speaking traveller, the Fat Tire Bike Tours aim to be fun and informative, with each guide sharing their own fascinating anecdotes rather than overloading you with a history book of dates. The company offers bicycle expeditions in cities throughout Europe, and in Paris there are tours of the city, Versailles and Monet's Gardens at Giverny.

With a picture of Monet's life forming in our minds, we alight at Vernon and walk to the morning farmers' market for picnic supplies. There is a small *marché* on Wednesday, but Saturday morning is the best time to come, when stallholders fill the town

squares. A visit provides an ideal opportunity to sample a diverse range of local farm produce and regional fare at its source. Deep in the rich Norman countryside, orchards of flowering apple trees spill down gently rolling hills and spotted cows graze peacefully on lush green pastures. The region is renowned for its apples as well as its milk, butter and cream, so it would be a shame not to sample the apple juice or cider and the delectable cow's milk cheeses – products which also make perfect picnic fare.

Normandy is home to four famous cheeses, all of which are protected by an AOP: *appellation d'origine protégé* (protected appellation of origin), formerly known as an AOC. When purchasing a product with this mark you are guaranteed that the food has been produced traditionally, in accordance with certain strict conditions. The mark also attests to the high quality of the product and its authenticity. Camembert de Normandie (as opposed to simply Camembert) is the most well-known of the four protected cheeses, or you may prefer to try soft, mild-flavoured Neufchâtel, often produced in a heart shape. Pont-l'Evêque comes in a square paver and has quite a strong aroma, and Livarot is a bitingly pungent cheese with an orange rind that I would rather not have sitting around in my backpack!

I wander around the market and choose a ripe round of Camembert de Normandie AOP, a thick slice of rabbit and cognac terrine, a few fat strawberries and a small bottle of cider before heading to Rose boulangerie and pâtisserie for a *Rétrodor* baguette and a fragrant apple and almond tartlet. (N.B. If you want to purchase half a baguette, as I did, boulangeries are quite happy to oblige. Ask for *une demi-baguette s'il vous plaît*.)

Then, with our goodies in our bags, we pick up our bikes, three-speed beach cruisers with fat tyres, and ride to the most idyllic picnic spot on the banks of the river Seine. We enjoy our picnic *en plein air* (in the open air), offering around hunks of cheese to try, wedges of crisp apple and summer cherries. Between the dozen of us we have a feast. I bite into my tart and watch the light play on the river as Kit gives us an overview of Impressionism as a movement, and its beginnings. He talks about Manet, whose unconventional scenes of real life and bold brushwork were an inspiration to the Impressionists, initiating a new freedom from traditional subjects. *Le déjeuner sur l'herbe* (Luncheon on the Grass), Manet's landmark painting of a modern-day female nude picnicking with two clothed men, shocked Paris critics and incensed the public.

As if on cue, we watch a skinny dipper brave the Seine.

Relaxed and happy from the sun and the cider, we hop back on our bikes and pedal down a private path to Monet's house and gardens. It's no Tour de France; rather a flat, easy ride past half-timbered houses and *clos normands* (walled Norman gardens) with roses in bloom. It makes me want to take the summer off and ride around the French countryside.

Before we know it, we have stepped into a Monet painting. Inside his *clos normand* is a sight to behold, a riot of beautiful flowers that tumble over pathways, climb up and over trellises and nod in the sun. Beds are organised by colour, like a fresh paint palette. The familiar pink storybook house with green shutters sits behind them, and a tunnel beneath the road leads to the waterlily pond with its arched Japanese bridge and softly trailing willows.

> 'Monet is the
> Raphael of water.'
>
> EDOUARD MANET

As time went by, the artist's beloved *nymphéas* (waterlilies) and Japanese-style lagoon became his sole source of inspiration, and he painted his water garden over and over, seeking to understand the changes in its reflection of the sky and capture every possible variation of light and movement, fascinated by

their transitory nature. Claude Monet moved to Giverny with his
family in May 1883 and lived here for forty-three years until his
death in 1926, aged eighty-six. He had a passion for gardening as
well as an obsession with colour, light and water, and both his
flower and water gardens, immortalised in so many of his paintings, became true works of art. The property was bequeathed by
Claude Monet's son Michael to the Académie des Beaux-Arts,
and was opened to the public in 1980 after careful restoration to
its original form.

Everywhere I look, there is a photo opportunity, a subject
to paint, beauty to admire. The property is open from 1 April to
1 November and right now in June *les jardins* are breathtaking,
but alas, it is also peak tourist season. Today there is a traffic jam
in Monet's gardens! This poses a quandary; do you visit when the
bright summer blooms 'pop' against a blue sky and the sun makes
a picnic more memorable, or when the gardens are a little more
tranquil? I have made the trip on several
occasions and find that no matter when I
visit, there is unfailingly a display, a living
painting. It's a garden lover's paradise,
where each month and season has its
own merit, and as Kit says, 'An overcast
day only serves to gives a dreamy, floaty
quality to the gardens that fits with the
Impressionist style.' In early spring the first snowdrops, daffodils
and tulips appear, and soon after, peonies and forget-me-nots
before the wisteria blossoms. Next come corn poppies and phlox,
and water irises on the edge of the pond. By summer, a riot of
hollyhocks, sweet peas and roses flank the laneways and perfume
the air, and lastly, asters and autumn hues.

'My garden is my most
beautiful masterpiece.'

'Colour is my day-long
obsession, joy and torment.'

CLAUDE MONET

Visitors can also tour the interior of the house and admire
Monet's extraordinary collection of Japanese woodcuts and

prints, surprise treasures reflecting his love of Japan that directly influenced his waterlily pond. Upstairs, from Monet's bedroom, is a glorious view over the gardens, while downstairs, the original copper pots still hang in the country kitchen and the sunny yellow dining room tricks one into thinking that the family will be home in time for dinner. Indeed, if you close your eyes to the crowds you can still feel the soul of the Monet family and the rhythm

of their daily life. It's not hard to visualise the atmosphere of this warm home filled with eight boisterous children, Monet working in his studio and garden, and the smell of *sole à la normande* coming from the kitchen. The couple had a passion for good food and there was a steady supply of fresh produce from their kitchen garden, apple orchard and farmyard, as well as from the Vernon market. Their *tarte Tatin* recipe was apparently a souvenir of visits to the Tatin sisters themselves, where they sampled this famous apple dish. The Monets also liked to receive friends, many of whom were leading figures of the time, and around their dining table they entertained not only the Impressionists but the likes of Rodin and Whistler.

The pretty little village of Giverny has many local artists' *ateliers* and galleries as well as the Musée des Impressionnismes. Formerly the 'Museum of American Art in Giverny', this new museum is dedicated to the history and impact of Impressionism, both in France and internationally, with particular attention to the Giverny colony and artists of the Seine Valley.

Before we meet back at the bikes, I relax with *une San Pé* (a San Pellegrino) on the shady terrace of the Ancien Hôtel Baudy. The mythical Baudy was often referred to as 'The American Painter's Hotel', as it attracted a flourishing colony of young American artists eager to set up their easels *en plein air* and put Impressionism into practice in the Norman landscape. Many artists gathered at the Baudy to present their work, gain inspiration and drink whisky, often leaving paintings to pay the rent. Afterwards, I slip through the hotel, now a café-restaurant, and into its enchanting back garden. A quiet corner of peace, it's fragrant with myriad varieties of old roses and rustic perennials. Up a flight of stone steps is a preserved nineteenth-century artist's studio.

Back on our bikes, we pause to pay our respects at Monet's grave in the village church grounds. He was buried beside the rest of his family, and the gravesite itself is planted with a small 'Monet's garden', a fitting tribute to a great man who loved flowers and colour. As we pedal along the path to Vernon, I reflect on what an enjoyable day it has been. Not only has the outing provided a welcome break from the hustle and bustle of Paris, but with a knowledgeable and passionate commentator, I have learnt so much more about Monet than on previous visits to Giverny.

We sink into our train seats and I get talking to Kit about food. He tells me he lives near the Rue des Entrepreneurs in the 15th arrondissement with his Iranian wife. 'A lot of Iranians live in the area and our favourite Persian

Artists studio at Ancien Hôtel Baudy

Ancien Hôtel
Baudy

restaurant is Mazeh on the Rue des Entrepreneurs.' This simple eatery and caterer is widely recognised for cooking some of the best Iranian food in Paris. 'Across the street from Mazeh are some Iranian grocery stores that have faloodeh to take home, but we prefer to eat it at Mazeh after a meal,' says Kit. Faloodeh is a deliciously refreshing Persian sorbet made with rosewater, cornstarch vermicelli noodles and sugar, and laced with lemon or lime juice. Another little patch of Paris to explore.

Kit also tells me he loves to go to vides-greniers (literally, empty attics). These neighbourhood garage sales are a community event. Streets are lined with tables, and a mix of merchants and families buy space and sell everything from vintage linen and clothes to books, jewellery and bric-a-brac. It's like one enormous garage sale! Roving *brocante* fairs are also very popular with the locals, and many prefer them to the renowned flea market at Porte de Clignancourt, simply known as *Les Puces* (The Fleas), which has become expensive, touristy and overwhelming on weekends. What Kit also finds endearing about the *vides-greniers* is the camaraderie brought about by food. Families and friends join together around tables to share a wonderful impromptu lunch while selling their wares. It's like having an opportunity to peek into the dining rooms of Paris.

Monet fans who can't make the day trip to Giverny shouldn't despair. Paris has the largest collections of works by Monet (and the other Impressionists) of any city in the world. My favourite place to see his paintings is in a beautiful townhouse in the 16th arrondissement. The Musée Marmottan, a former hunting lodge next to the Bois de Boulogne, provides respite from the crowds of the larger, more well-known city institutions. Not to be underestimated, this intimate museum offers the world's largest collection of Monets under one roof, including a waterlily series. You will also find Monet's *Impression, Sunrise* – the painting that gave the Impressionist movement its name; works by Morisot, Sisley, Pissaro and Gauguin; and a collection of sculptures. Combine a visit with a shopping spree on the nearby Rue de Passy. Crammed with chic boutiques, this blue-ribbon street

is the centre of life in the elegant residential quarter of Passy. Whatever you do, don't miss Aux Merveilleux de Fred on the little market street off Rue de Passy – as marvellous as it sounds! Fred concentrates on just one thing: meringues. From outside you can watch through the window as the flat, crunchy wheels with soft centres are made, layered and decorated. Big bowls are filled with white clouds and fluffy cream, and spatulas work overtime. The snowball-sized creations are perfect for a snack and come in just three flavours: chocolate, coffee and spéculoos (spiced biscuit crumbs). After being cloaked in cream they are rolled in dark chocolate shavings, crystals of coffee or spéculoos and white chocolate. Which to choose? I'll leave you with that dilemma.

Another must-see for Monet fans is the Musée de l'Orangerie in the corner of the Jardin des Tuileries. It houses a series of eight enormous waterlily paintings displayed in two serene oval rooms. Some of Monet's most abstract works hang here, and with natural light filtering through from above, they take on an almost ethereal quality, the mood of the room changing with the time of day. In peak tourist season, beware, queues are long, so aim to arrive early in order to truly meditate on these dream-like canvases. Fans of Impressionism will also appreciate the Walter-Guillaume collection in the basement, with masterpieces by Cézanne and Renoir. Conveniently, the museum is situated close by the gorgeous tea salon, Ladurée (see page 22), also best visited in the morning to avoid a queue. You can't visit Paris without sampling their magical macarons!

Finally, on the banks of the Seine, in a former train station, the Musée d'Orsay contains France's greatest collection of Impressionist art, with notable works by Renoir, Manet, Degas, Sisley and Pissaro, as well as Monet. Here you will find his *Blue Waterlilies; Poppy Field;* and *London, The Parliament: A Gap of Sunlight in the Fog.* After viewing his masterpieces, be sure to treat yourself to afternoon tea in the elegant Belle Epoque restaurant on the first floor. Resplendent with ornate ceiling frescoes, crystal chandeliers and arched windows overlooking the Seine, it's a perfect museum break. Also hanging on these walls are *La Gare Saint-Lazare* and fragments of Monet's monumental version of *Le Déjeuner sur l'Herbe* (Luncheon on the Grass), inspired by Manet's original, which also hangs here. All three shall always be reminders of my lovely day trip to the Normandy countryside. ◊

PARIS BY MOUTH >>

Paris by Mouth is the most wonderful website. Reviews are gathered from a stable of established food writers who spend their days tucking in their serviettes and tasting delicious morsels. The site is edited by professional food writers, and it works *comme ça*: 'We take the words that are scattered all over the web, filter out the junk, and present it in a way that helps you follow the trends and find a place to eat tonight.' With a collection of exceptional addresses at their fingertips, it makes sense that these experienced local food writers would use their knowledge to lead tours focusing exclusively on food and wine, which is exactly what they have recently done.

These delicious crawls, with generous tastings included, introduce participants to a trail of treats from artisan breads, cheese, wine and charcuterie to mouth-watering gateaux, chocolate and ice cream. You may like to explore the specialist food shops of the 'gastronomically gifted' Saint-Germain area, or perhaps climb up to Montmartre, where behind the sugary domes of Sacré-Cœur a creative community go about their daily life in the vibrant Abbesses quarter. The Best of Montmartre food tour will take you to tucked-away artisan food shops and to a baker who won the prize for La Meilleure (best) Baguette de Paris.

There are also specialised tours. The cheese-obsessed can sign up for the Tour de Fromage, wine lovers can join La Revolution du Vin and sip natural wines in trendy eastern Paris, and dessert fans need look no further than Sweet Paris: The Chocolate and Pastry Extravaganza. Tours run almost daily and can be booked online.

Paris by Mouth | Visit www.parisbymouth.com to learn more.

ADDRESSES

Ancien Hôtel Baudy
81, Rue Claude Monet,
27620, Giverny
☎ 02 32 21 10 03

Fat Tire Bike Tours
24, Rue Edgar Faure, 75015
☎ 01 56 58 10 54
www.FatTireBikeTours.com/Paris
N.B. Monet's garden tour: market
visit on Saturday only.

Fondation/House
and Gardens of
Claude Monet
84, Rue Claude Monet,
27620, Giverny
☎ 02 32 51 28 21
www.fondation-monet.com

Mazeh
65, Rue des Entrepreneurs
☎ 01 45 75 33 89
www.mazeh.com

Aux Merveilleux de Fred
29, Rue de l'Annonciation, 75016
☎ 01 45 20 13 82
www.auxmerveilleux.com

Musée de l'Orangerie
Jardin des Tuileries, 75001
☎ 01 44 77 80 07
www.musee-orangerie.fr

Musée Marmottan-
Claude Monet
2, Rue Louis-Boilly, 75016
☎ 01 44 96 50 33
www.marmottan.com

Musée des
Inpressionnismes
99, Rue Claude Monet,
27620, Giverny
☎ 02 32 51 94 65
www.mdig.fr

Musée d'Orsay
62, Rue de Lille, 75007
☎ 01 40 49 48 14
www.musee-orsay.fr

Rose
74, Rue Albufera, 27200, Vernon
☎ 02 32 51 03 98
www.boulangerie-rose-vernon.fr

Vides-greniers
and brocantes
www.vide-greniers.org
www.brocabrac.fr

CHAPTER SIX

Mint Tea &
HONEY

♦♦♦

Notre-Dame

SEINE

BD. SAINT-GERMAIN

Musée National
du Moyen Age

6e

Terroir
Parisien

Musée
National
d'Histoir
Naturel

Le Jardin du
Luxembourg

RUE SAINT-JACQUES

Arènes
de Lutèce

Le
Jardin
des
Plantes

BD. SAINT-MICHEL

Hammam de la Mosquée

La Grande
Mosquée de
Paris

N

5e

La Tuile à Loup

The Cluny is one of my favourite small museums in Paris, the flamboyant building itself a stirring and rare example of secular Gothic style. The ogee arches, turrets and dragon gargoyles make it hard to believe there's not a princess locked up at the top of the spiral staircase in the five-sided tower. Gateways are edged with angels holding scrolls, cornices decorated with imaginary beasts. If you look closely, you will find gables stamped with a tiny monkey or a cat washing its face, and little figures riding dolphins and snails.

The Cluny

In the heart of the Latin Quarter at the foot of the Sainte-Geneviève hill, this romantic private mansion was built by the Cluny abbots in the fifteenth century and sits atop the remains of Gallo-Roman thermal baths. Together, they make a unique setting for the collections officially known as the Musée National du Moyen Age, the Museum of the Middle Ages.

Inside, it's full of bygone treasures, a medieval attic offering valuable insight into the art and life of the period. From exquisite stained-glass windows, sculptures, paintings and enamels to items used in everyday life, there are so many wonderful things here that I can't help but return again and again. My friend Pam is similarly struck by the Cluny, and when I mentioned I was visiting this morning and asked if she'd like to join me for a day in the Latin Quarter, she was powerless to say no. The fact that we have previously made this pilgrimage together and know the collection quite well adds another dimension of pleasure to our visit.

'A walk about Paris will provide lessons in history, beauty, and in the point of life.'

THOMAS JEFFERSON

Pam and I wander through the rooms and down to the vestiges of the baths, the finest Roman remains in Paris, which were once a remarkable maze of cold, tepid and hot rooms and pools. One can only imagine the splendour of the original decorations; walls were faced with coloured stone and nautical mosaics, and even the tubs were made of white marble. We reacquaint ourselves with *The Golden Rose*, a long-stemmed bunch of roses made of gold for the Pope in the thirteenth century; the sculpted heads of Saint Denis; archers' shields and the narwhal horn; but the highlight for us both is the celebrated *Lady and the Unicorn* tapestries – *La Dame à la Licorne*.

Ablaze with rich colours, the pieces are exquisite examples of the *millefleurs*-style tapestries. Five are allegorical illustrations of the senses and the mysterious sixth represents love and understanding. Spellbindingly beautiful, each tapestry depicts a woman with flowing golden hair standing on a floating royal-blue island, with thousands of tiny, perfectly detailed flowers in the deep red background. Flanked by a lion and a unicorn, the lady's surrounds are alive with scampering foxes and leopards. Mesmerised all over again, we emerge into the bright light outside and tour the medieval-themed garden. Across the road in Square Paul-Painlevé is the *millefleurs* flower bed, drawing inspiration from the tapestries.

Terroir Parisien, Yannick Alléno

We tear ourselves from the Middle Ages and walk a few blocks to Rue Saint Victor. I have booked a table at Terroir Parisien for lunch. Under the guidance of dedicated locavore Yannick

Alléno, this stylish new bistro in the Latin Quarter showcases
food locally grown and produced in Ile-de-France (Paris and

its environs). Culinary history is also
honoured, and this native of the region is
passionate about bringing back old dishes
and forgotten recipes as well as featuring
rare produce that has all but vanished
from local tables. 'Everything is from Île de
France, has a history, or originated here,'
says the waiter. Alléno's revival of cooking
with produce from the region sprouted
when the three-Michelin-star chef created
a popular *Terroir Parisien* lunch menu at
the luxury Hôtel Meurice. (Alléno has
recently left the Meurice to pursue a new
culinary vision at Le 1947, a two-Michelin-
star restaurant in the alpine chalet, Cheval
Blanc, at Courchevel.) The modern bistro
is light and airy with an open kitchen,

dark wood and a natural feel. Around the walls are crates of
vegetables, displays of local produce and a list of Alléno's sources
and suppliers. Top-notch ingredients come from the best
growers and small farmers in and around the Paris region, from
fruit and vegetables to lamb and beef. Mint is from Milly-la-forêt,
peaches from Montreuil and asparagus from Argenteuil. Back
on the menu is Pontoise cabbage, an ancient variety of purple
cabbage depicted by the Impressionist painter Camille Pissarro
in *Cabbage Field, Pontoise*. Alléno is even reviving a rare breed
of chickens called *Poularde de Houdan*. These Houdan hens,
recognised by their black plumage mottled with white and
a butterfly-shaped crest, were highly esteemed for their meat in
the late nineteenth century.

Dishes are surprisingly simple and pared back, in homage to their true origins. Open seven days a week, you can crunch into a croque-monsieur at the bar with a relaxing glass of wine at any time of the day. There are plates of charcuterie from the esteemed Gilles Vérot, and *gratinée 'des Halles'*. For entrée I tuck into a classic *salade de frisée, cresson à l'œuf mollet et croutons et lardons:* curly endive and watercress topped with a perfectly wobbly, soft-cooked egg, crispy croutons and rustic slabs of salty bacon. Pam starts with *une salade Parisienne*: a simple salad of butter lettuce with good ham, new potatoes, boiled eggs and gruyère tossed in mustard vinaigrette.

On the short and meaty mains menu, today's special is *une blanquette de veau à l'ancienne* and there's also French beef in a white wine and shallot 'sauce Bercy', named after the historic quarter in eastern Paris that was once one of the largest wine-trading centres in Europe. A number of historic dishes on the menu hark back to the days when the bounty on the Parisian table mostly came from the surrounding land, and each product and dish has a story. I opt for skate with capers in a toasty, hazelnut-brown butter sauce, with a side dish of spinach from Montfermeil. There is an assortment of cheese from the region and for dessert, *brioche 'Nanterre' perdu, glace vanille* (brioche French toast with vanilla ice cream), or a poached pear with *Miel Béton* – yes, 'cement' honey! The beehives are in the city.

Terroir Parisien received a Bib Gourmand Michelin 2013. These *Bonnes Petites Tables* (good little tables) have a book of their own, and are defined as the inspectors' 'favourite addresses for good value', showcasing good cuisine at reasonable prices.

After lunch, we meander towards the tranquil Jardin des Plantes, an oft-overlooked corner of the Latin Quarter. Along the way, we peek into the remains of the Arènes de Lutèce, constructed at the end of the first century. A public park with

kids kicking soccer balls, this vast Roman amphitheatre was once the venue for gladiator fights. Today, it is used by theatre companies and for demonstrations.

A rambling patch of green in central Paris, the Jardin des Plantes is an enchanting spot to catch your breath and connect with nature. Gardeners are working away, their wheelbarrows are full, and bees are buzzing about beds of colourful summer flowers. The botanical gardens were created as a royal medicinal herb garden at the instigation of the physicians of Louis XIII, and opened to the public in 1640. There are rose, iris and alpine gardens, ancient archways of shady trees and glasshouses that will take you either to the tropics or to hot, dry lands. Today, the 'botanical garden' features thousands of varieties of medicinal plants. My favourite plot is the sunny potager, with ancient and modern varieties of fruits and vegetables.

A large, sprawling park, it also encompasses the National Museum of Natural History, a school of botany and the menagerie. One of the oldest zoos in the world, it was set up during the French Revolution to house the surviving animals from Versailles' royal menagerie. Circus animals and exotic creatures were added, but at the time of the Prussian siege of Paris in 1870, most ended up on the dinner plates of hungry Parisians. Nowadays, the menagerie focuses on endangered species and those of small size.

Jardin des Plantes

The towering minaret of the largest mosque in France, La Grande Mosquée de Paris, leads us to our next stop. We slip through a Moorish archway and into a courtyard shaded by trees and umbrellas. Amid lanterns and chirping birds, waiters glide by with trays of sweet mint tea in delicate glasses. Here in the mosque's North African café there is an immediate feeling of serenity. We sit and sip refreshing mint tea and bite into honey-soaked Algerian pastries. A group in the corner relax on cushions, smoking an Arabic water pipe, the scented shisha smoke drifting across our mosaic-topped table. Surely this is one of the most delightful and unusual spots for tea in the city, and pastries are just €2 each.

For an even more exotic experience, disappear into a cloud of steam at the mosque's hammam. These hushed baths, all marble, mosaics and trickling fountains, offer a chance to be transported to a world of hot steam rooms and cold plunge pools. A rub with black soap and a bracing *gommage* (a good ol' buff by your own private scrubber) will leave your skin shiny and new. Take note, this is a traditional steam bath, not a chic spa.

Moroccan, Algerian and Tunisian artisans built the pink marble mosque in the 1920s to honour French-Arab soldiers killed in World War I, and after tea, we take a wander around the public areas. Visitors are welcome as long as they are respectfully dressed. It's well worth even a glance through the entrance into the gorgeous interior garden with its peaceful fountains and stunning aqua Moroccan tiles. Short tours of the building are available from 9 a.m. to noon and 4 to 6 p.m., except Fridays, the Muslim holy day.

Here, Pam and I say our goodbyes until next time, and I walk along Rue Daubenton towards my final stop for the afternoon, La Tuile à Loup. Eric Goujou's colourful little shop near the Rue Mouffetard market street is stocked with some of the best hand-crafted objects in the country, made in the traditional way by provincial artisans. (If you're starting to drag your feet after a long day, drop into the store on a visit to this ancient market instead.) Most of the pieces are for the kitchen and table, and crafts from many regions of France are displayed on the wooden tables and shelves. Stock changes regularly. Today I find hand-blown glassware from Auvergne, block-printed linen from Provence, and earthenware from Provence or Burgundy. It's where you come for

La Grande
Mosquée de Paris

a rustic *cassole*, the traditional earthenware bowl used to serve cassoulet, or a Savoyard milk jug decorated with polka dots that traditionally represent the harvest moon. What I love most is the exquisite selection of handmade pottery, boldly coloured bowls, and plates and dishes with rich glazes and interesting patterns. Whether you snap up a fish-shaped platter or tureen topped with birds, these unique and practical reminders of France can be shipped worldwide.

La Tuile à Loup

I can't help but duck to the end of the street, just to drink in the life on the bustling Rue Mouffetard. The cobbled market street is a hive of activity and bursting with fresh, colourful produce. There are shiny olives, succulent prawns and mounds of summer strawberries just begging to be served on those bright plates and dishes. ◊

ADDRESSES

Café Maure de la Mosquée de Paris
39, Rue Geoffroy Saint-Hilaire, 75005
☎ 01 43 31 38 20

La Grande Mosquée de Paris
2 bis, Place du Puits-de-l'Ermite, 75005
☎ 01 45 35 97 33

Hammam de la Mosquée
39, Rue Geoffroy Saint-Hilaire 75005
☎ 01 43 31 18 14
(Separate days for men and women; check website for details. Enter through the back of the café.)
www.la-mosquee.com

Jardin des Plantes
57, Rue Cuvier, 75005

Musée National du Moyen Age
6, Place Paul-Painlevé, 75005
☎ 01 53 73 78 16
www.musee-moyenage.fr

Musée National d'Histoire Naturelle
36, Rue Geoffroy Saint-Hilaire, 75005
☎ 01 40 79 56 01
www.mnhn.fr

Terroir Parisien
25, Rue Saint Victor, 75005
☎ 01 44 31 54 54
www.yannick-alleno.com

La Tuile à Loup
35, Rue Daubenton, 75005
☎ 01 47 07 28 90
www.latuilealoup.com

CHAPTER SEVEN

La Fabuleuse Tarte AU CHOCOLAT

◆◆◆

It's mid-morning by the time I wend my way towards Rue Saint-Dominique for a late breakfast after a quick zip up the Eiffel Tower. There's nothing quite like the panoramic view from the top as the city stretches awake, and an early visit means you mostly beat the crowds. When our family lived in Paris, after countless visits with guests in tow, it got to the point where I could hardly bear to make the pilgrimage one more time. A decade on, I see the expedition in a magical new light. Standing on the breezy platform, with the Seine winding through the city below and Sacré-Cœur sitting high on the butte of Montmartre, it's impossible not to be wooed by the Iron Lady.

29, Avenue Rapp

I deviate a little on my way, to marvel at the door and façade of number 29, Avenue Rapp. Full of character and perhaps the best example of Art Nouveau architecture in Paris, the ceramics and brickwork sing and dance with motifs of female figures, animals and flowers. Created for the ceramist Alexandre Bigot, the erotic, Baroque-inspired work won his friend and designer, Jules Lavirotte, first prize in the 1901 *Concours des Façades de la Ville de Paris*. Viewing it for the first time will leave you open-mouthed. Take time to savour the details, including the fox fur around the neck of the woman in the carving above the door, said to be a portrait of Lavirotte's wife.

A few steps on, another fine example of Lavirotte's work can be found at 3, Square Rapp, an eccentric building with unusual decorative features, elaborate balconies, and even a watch-tower. From the lavish iron gate there is a dazzling view of the Eiffel Tower. So many side streets in the beau 7th arrondisse-ment reveal an unexpected flash of the iconic structure. I remember my youngest daughter asking as we drove through the streets one day, 'How many Eiffel Towers *are* there in Paris, Mummy?'

I soon turn left on to Rue Saint-Dominique, an elegant street that arches gracefully across the 7th, connecting Parc du Champ de Mars to Les Invalides. Poodles rule the footpaths, flowers tumble from window boxes and it's chock-full of superb places to eat. Affectionately dubbed 'Rue Constant', the street is worth a detour just to dine at one of three restaurants that Christian Constant runs or oversees, all with their own distinct character and cuisine. One of the most famous chefs in France, Constant started his career as an apprentice at the age of fourteen and went on to train a whole new generation of chefs. In 1998, he left his position as Executive Chef at Les Ambassadeurs at the Hôtel de Crillon and crossed the river to open his first restaurant, Le Violon d'Ingres. His aim was to create a friendly, unpretentious neighbourhood restaurant with comforting yet sophisticated French food. Today this lovely spot with superb seasonal dishes is a popular choice for a special meal that's both creative and not too formal. Stylish, contemporary and filled with light, the one-Michelin-star restaurant has recently been refurbished.

Café Constant

But this morning it is Café Constant, another of his addresses, that I am heading for. Madelyn, the friendly American I have come to meet, has already ordered the *formule express* when I arrive: coffee, freshly squeezed orange juice, yoghurt and a buttery, flaky croissant delivered from a local pâtisserie. I pull up a chair. Open all day, it's stitched tightly into the tasteful fabric of this residential neighbourhood, and is not only a good spot for a coffee and croissant before or after a jaunt to the Eiffel Tower, but also for a casual lunch or dinner. Although it's close to *la tour Eiffel*, it manages to stay off the immediate tourist radar. The traditional bistro dishes are made to Constant's grandmother's recipes in a classic setting that hasn't changed since the 1950s.

As we enjoy our *petit déjeuner*, Madelyn tells me all about Paris Perfect, the company she started fifteen years ago with her French husband and former cardiac surgeon, Philippe, as a way of sharing their love for the city. Paris Perfect offers hand-selected luxury rentals with fully remodelled kitchens and bathrooms on light-filled upper floors. All of the apartments are in quarters with a neighbourhood feel. Many, in fact, are right here in the surrounding streets, with stunning views of the Eiffel Tower.

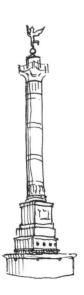

In the heart of the Left Bank, this chic part of town boasts an idyllic central location and is one of the city's most desirable residential pockets, with a mix of classic old apartments and elegant village-like streets. It is also walking distance to several impressive monuments and museums. Smacking of old money and simmering with discreet good taste, this district is home to many old Parisian families as well as an alarming number of gorgeous florist shops and cosy neighbourhood restaurants. In addition, there is a bounty of gourmet delights, making it an ideal locale for food lovers to spoil themselves by renting

an apartment. Freed from the limitations of a hotel room, an apartment provides the opportunity to live like a true (if rather privileged) Parisian, falling in step with the rituals of everyday life. Such joy comes from nicking down to *la boulangerie* early in the morning to return with a bag of warm, sweet-scented pastries, or filling your basket at the market before heading home for an al fresco lunch on the balcony.

'I ought to be jealous of the tower. She is more famous than I am.'

GUSTAVE EIFFEL

After breakfast, Madelyn has to check on the workmen at her latest remodel around the corner, and I tag along for a look. Even unfinished, with a drill whizzing and dust swirling, this seventh-floor apartment named Margaux is, quite simply, heaven. It boasts three bedrooms, two bathrooms, a superb kitchen, and the largest wrap-around balcony of all their rentals. Soon, lucky guests will be able to live the dream of *la vie parisienne*. It will have dress-circle seats, and I can only imagine how extraordinary the setting must be as the sun sets over the Paris rooftops and the Eiffel Tower puts on her magic shows, bursting to life with thousands of twinkling lights.

I leave Madelyn and head towards Rue Cler market street, scouting out a couple of restaurants she has recommended on the way. Seriously close to the Eiffel Tower, Au Petit Sud Ouest specialises in duck. It's the place to come for artisanal foie gras from the Landes region (tables are equipped with toasters so you can make your own hot toast), a good *magret de canard* with crispy potatoes, and a glass of Bordeaux. The other little spot is FL, tucked down a quiet street with just twenty-five seats. It's too early for service but the two guys inside open the door for a chat. Pots bubble away in the little open kitchen. I am excited to discover that both have worked for Tony Bilson in Sydney. FL (a word play on Eiffel) emphasises cuisine from Picardy in northern

View from 'Margaux' apartment, Paris Perfect

France, chef Nicolas Valanchon's home region. Few Parisian restaurants focus on the region, so this makes a pleasant change. The quietly spoken chef says he uses Picardy products when he can, and the menu, which is very affordable for this part of town, changes with the market.

One of the advantages of the 7th is the abundance of open-air markets and green space in and around the arrondissement, providing plenty of opportunities to shop on foot for fresh, seasonal produce and to picnic. Marché Saxe-Breteuil, a large market with a lively country village atmosphere, has set up its colourful striped canopies under the long shadow of the Eiffel Tower since 1873, and Marché President Wilson (see page 165) springs up twice a week just across the river.

> 'Though I often looked for one, I finally had to admit that there could be no cure for Paris.'
>
> FROM *THE PARIS WIFE,*
> PAULA MCLAIN

Rue Cler is in full swing, poodles yapping, when I arrive. This traditional merchant street is a favourite food destination in the quarter where locals converge to meet friends over *un café* and fill their baskets with high-quality produce. On warm summer days, you can smell the sweet fragrance of strawberries and apricots in the air as you walk along this pedestrianised street, perhaps with a homemade ice cream from Martine Lambert's parlour. The cheery bunches of flowers make me want to fill a vase and fling open my French doors while the pristine fish at La Sablaise Poissonnerie sparkle on beds of ice, ready for a hot pan of butter. Out the front, there are wicker baskets of *bulots* (whelks), *tourteaux* (the highly regarded European crab) from the north-east Atlantic coast and live lobsters. Many fishmongers in Paris will clean and cook your lobster for you. All you have to do is return to pick it up.

Rue Cler

My favourite store on the street, however, has always been the deliciously tempting Davoli. Drawing a loyal local clientele,

this exceptional Italian *charcuterie* will have you drooling and dreaming of a picnic. Inside, it's cluttered with legs of *jambon de Parme*, terrines and tapenades as well as fine Italian sausage, cheese, wine and truffles. There are soft pillows of ravioli and bright antipasti. A variety of classic prepared dishes are made daily and sold on the terrace, a boon for busy gourmands in holiday mode. Especially on a cold day, the mingling aromas of these inviting, hot dishes rouse a hearty appetite and make Davoli near-impossible to pass without stopping. Depending on the season, you may find *lapin aux pruneaux* (rabbit with prunes), tomatoes *à la Provençale*, a golden gratin of courgettes or osso buco. Perfect to take home to your apartment! Then, of course, there are the sweet Italian pastries to nibble with coffee

Café du Marché

or perhaps some cherry *clafoutis* to serve warm with a dollop of cream. Typically, traditional Limousin *clafoutis* contains the cherry pits, left in for the subtle almond flavour they impart.

Just around the corner, past the ever-popular Café du Marché with its sweeping terrace, is Marie-Anne Cantin's *fromagerie*. Cantin is passionate about traditional methods of cheese-making, and trades in artisan cheeses from personally selected farms, which are then aged in the cellar beneath the shop.

It's after one when I arrive at Christian Constant's third address, Les Cocottes, for lunch and join the queue of locals waiting for a table in the long, narrow dining room. The casual eatery is chic and modern with high wooden benches and comfy stools, and on this beautiful crisp day it's welcoming and warm. Shelves around the walls are stacked with preserves and Constant's

cookbooks and cocottes are available for purchase. What's a cocotte, you ask? It's an oven-to-table pot with a lid, or an individual ramekin or skillet used for baking and serving. In keeping with the concept of the restaurant, many of the comforting choices arrive in enamelled cast-iron Staub pots and dishes, designed to enhance flavour as well as retain heat. Known for its simple, delicious dishes, the restaurant also serves soups and salads and scrumptious desserts, and the menu changes each season.

Soon I have a seat, and it's one of those places where you feel perfectly happy dining alone. Today there's an enticing *velouté de champignons, crème de chantilly parfumé au foie gras*: a silky mushroom soup with chantilly cream flavoured with foie gras, but I opt to start with the *jambon de Pays Basque* from the renowned artisan charcuterie Chez Ospital, served with chewy country bread and a glass of Bourgogne Côtes d'Auxerre 2012. With its relaxed atmosphere, friendly staff, excellent service and good value, it hits the spot for a quick yet impressive lunch, but as there's a no-reservations policy, it's probably best to arrive close to the beginning of service.

For main course, I opt for the Cocotte du Jour, *Boulette d'agneau aux épices*, with a glass of Rasteau Côtes de Rhone 2012 AOP. Perhaps the tastiest meatballs I've had the pleasure of eating, they are served atop a creamy mousseline of potatoes, the aroma of the spices and sauce hitting the senses at once when you lift the lid. Beautifully presented, this is good, honest and tasty French cooking. How can I possibly leave without sampling *la fabuleuse tarte au chocolat de Christian Constant,* which lives up to its name? I finish with an espresso served with *une petite cuillère Poilâne,* a crisp teaspoon-shaped biscuit made by the famous bakery. Revived, I step back out on to the street and continue walking down Rue Saint-Dominique.

Generous at heart, Constant has a reputation of helping those he trains buy into restaurants. Originally run by Constant, the intimate Les Fables de la Fontaine just a few doors up is now in the capable hands of his protégés, Sébastien Gravé and David Bottreau, former chef and maître d'hôtel of Le Violon d'Ingres. This unique and excellent fish restaurant on a pleasant little square is an address to keep on ice. The Michelin one-star has a modern, convivial atmosphere, and just a dozen tables. The menu is small and inventive, and the seafood dishes well prepared, focusing on the catch of the day. Desserts are also delicious. At a recent dinner with my friend Jocelyn we finished with a warm black cherry jam *gâteau basque,* with two exquisite scoops of vanilla ice cream – and two spoons. It's a little pricey, and in true French style, elbow to elbow, but in summer, if you reserve ahead, you can dine on the small cobbled square facing the fountain.

On the other side of the square is yet another good address. (If you rent an apartment nearby you may never leave the quarter!). A longstanding favourite, the charming La Fontaine de Mars with its red-and-white-chequered tablecloths, clanging kitchen bell and traditional cuisine from the south-west was named after the small fountain on the square. Commissioned by Napoleon, *la fontaine* was originally used as a watering place for horses. The tables set up in fine weather under the pretty stone arcade are coveted by local residents and visitors alike, who come to tuck in to seasonal bistro fare.

I continue down Rue Saint-Dominique but it's difficult to make headway as the side street, Rue Jean Nicot, has more delights. Fresh garden flowers spill over the pavement at the striking little florist shop Un Jour de Fleurs. One of the darlings of the Parisian flower world and popular with the fashion industry, Eric Chauvin's hallmarks are simplicity, romance and elegance. His eye for natural beauty shines through and his creations often feature masses of irises, roses and peonies. You'll also find his flowers at Le Violon d'Ingres. Two doors up is the whimsical Belle Epoque bakery, Stéphane Secco, iced in dreamy pink. The window beckons with savoury tarts: *pissaliadière*, *piperade à la tomate* and golden quiches, while inside it's all painted tiles and mirrors. A crowd clamours to choose from Secco's excellent breads and pastries. Moist, sticky madeleines vie with tangy lemon tartlets, financiers and macarons. The wide selection of salads, baguette sandwiches and fruit tarts makes this an ideal spot to pick up supplies on a sunny day before picnicking on the banks of the Seine or in the back garden of the Rodin Museum, which is where I am heading.

Directly opposite Rue Jean Nicot on the southern side of Rue

Stéphane Secco

Saint-Dominique is Passage Jean Nicot, an ancient, shadowy passageway that draws you in like a good mystery book. It's a worthwhile diversion, for across Rue de Grenelle at the end of the passageway is the sweetest little church set in the sleepy Square Saint-Jean Denys Bühler, complete with an half-timbered house. A little-known patch of peace.

From here I continue down Rue de Grenelle, passing through the expansive Les Invalides. This imposing complex encompasses the grand Hôtel des Invalides, gardens and several museums including the Musée de l'Armée, the world's greatest military museum. The vast building with objects dating back to the Vikings is best left for a free afternoon. Even if militaria is not your thing, it's hard not to be fascinated by one of the world's largest collections of medieval armour and the bugle used to call the armistice in 1918. The complex also features the Sun King's Dome Church. It is here in the crypt that Napoleon rests under a gilded cupola that sparkles on the skyline like a giant Fabergé egg.

The Sun King's Dome church

More my thing is the Musée Rodin, possibly the most romantic museum in Paris and a wonderful escape from the busy city streets. Suddenly, I am surrounded by secret pathways and quiet, cool corners in which to contemplate masterpieces such as *The Thinker, Monument to Balzac* and *The Gates of Hell*. Particularly in the spring and summertime,

'I choose a block of marble and chop off whatever I don't need.'

AUGUSTE RODIN

the garden (which can be visited independently for just €2) is a true oasis and a must-see, with hundreds of fragrant rose bushes, rows of leafy lime trees and a tranquil pond. Auguste Rodin lived and worked here in the last years of his life and almost 400 of his works are displayed in the garden and splendid eighteenth-century mansion, where you will find *The Kiss*.

I would have a coffee in the outdoor café if it weren't for the pesky pigeons. Just as well that one street over there's a café that serves some of the best coffee in the city. Dreaming of a good strong latte, a rarity in Paris, I stride down Boulevard des Invalides

and turn left on to Rue de Babylone. As I reach number 57 bis (57B), I pause to admire La Pagode, as I always do when I pass this way. Surely one of the most magical arthouse cinemas in the world, this flamboyant nineteenth-century replica of an oriental pagoda is refreshingly out of place in the classically dressed 7th. It was commissioned by Monsieur Morin, the director of Le Bon Marché department store, in the 1890s, as an exotic gift for his wife when all things oriental were in vogue. Constructed in their garden, it became an enchanting venue for sumptuous receptions until Madame Morin left her husband for his associate. *One Mad Kiss* inaugurated La Pagode as a film theatre in 1931 and it became a 'cinema temple' for showing the best foreign films.

La Pagode

Jean Cocteau gave the first screening of *Le Testament d'Orphée* here in 1959. La Pagode has two screening rooms but the one to opt for is the exuberant and heavily decorated Salle Japonaise,

complete with chandeliers, exquisite carvings, wall hangings and frescoes of warrior scenes. Tea is served in the oriental-style front garden in summer and in the little tea room in winter, but it's coffee that I want and I'm just a few steps from Coutume.

There's no doubt there has been a blind spot when it comes to coffee in Paris, especially a good espresso with steamed milk. Strange, really, considering the city's food and wine reputation and obsession with quality. Perhaps it's because the Parisian coffee culture is more about hanging out on the terrace than what's in the cup, which is sometimes undrinkable. Thankfully, Tom Clark and Antoine Netien, the founders of Coutume, are part of a new wave bringing Paris coffee out of the dark ages and into the spotlight, teaming up to produce their own brand and roastery. I sit and chat with Tom, a young Aussie, while sipping a hot and strong creamy latte.

After spending a year in France, Tom realised there was a gap in the market. France did not offer the barista-style brews and serious artisan coffee he was used to; in fact, it was decades behind. 'Sydney has around twelve hundred roasters, while Paris has approximately ten,' says Tom. Back from training in Melbourne, a city with a cutting-edge coffee scene, his French business partner and master *torréfacteur* (roaster) Antoine Netien saw the future and they decided to team up. After extensive research, and travelling through Europe to meet with roasters, they opened the café in 2011. Coutume is also committed to education and training, with public tastings as well as barista courses, so hopefully it won't be long before welcome changes percolate through Paris. 'Our aim is to revitalise as well as enrich French coffee culture,' says Tom. This afternoon, business is brisk. 'We attract traditional French families from the area as well as students and the international community. Saturday and Sunday brunch are very busy,' says Clark. There's a light menu with an emphasis on natural flavours and colours, healthy foods and vegetarian dishes, as well as bio juices and smoothies. Pastries are from the fabulous Pâtisserie des Rêves (see page 187). Good coffee and a perfect pastry – a marriage made in seventh heaven. ◊

O CHATEAU >>

For an interesting apéro before dinner and splendid views, book a Champagne Cruise on the Seine with **O Chateau**. Leaving at 6 p.m. from near the Eiffel Tower, the one-hour tour takes you past the monuments of Paris, around the islands and under the bridges while you taste and learn about three different Champagnes from a sommelier. There's a bit of chit-chat about the history of Champagne and method of production, but not so much as to distract you from the next bridge coming up as you sip and sightsee. You gain a perspective from the water that you just cannot get from land as you pass sculptures, fishermen and fanciful iron work. The tasting is conducted in a private salon at the front of the boat, with a private deck.

For visitors who yearn to learn more about French wine, O Chateau has a range of tours and classes, or you can simply drop in to their wine bar and restaurant. Here you will find a fantastic team of friendly and passionate people who all speak excellent English and are trained wine experts. Between them, they seem to have worked in wine regions all over the world. As well as good-quality restaurant food, there are boards of charcuterie and cheese available if you just want to hang out at the bar and taste some great French wines. There are three pours: 30, 100 and 150 mls, and the selection of wines by the glass change weekly.

Classes are conducted in two tasting rooms on the premises. Amongst the sessions on offer are a Wine and Cheese Lunch and a Grand Cru Tasting. There is also a day trip to the Champagne region. It's an easygoing and fun day with no script and lots of tasting. Lunch is at a winery with the winemaker.

O Chateau | 68, Rue Jean-Jacques Rousseau, 75001 | ☎ 01 44 73 97 80 | www.o-chateau.com

Pont Alexandre III

ADDRESSES

Café Constant

139, Rue Saint-Dominique, 75007
No reservations. Open 7 days a
week from 8.30 a.m. to
11 p.m.
www.parisperfect.com

Les Cocottes

135, Rue Saint-Dominique, 75007
No reservations. Open 7 days a
week midday to 4 p.m. and
7 p.m. to 10.30 p.m.

Coutume

47, Rue de Babylone, 75007
☎ 01 45 51 50 47
www.coutumecafe.com

Davoli

34, Rue Cler, 75007
☎ 01 45 51 23 41
www.davoli.fr

Les Fables
de la Fontaine

131, Rue Saint-Dominique, 75007
☎ 01 44 18 37 55
lesfablesdelafontaine.net

FL

1 bis, Rue Augereau, 75007
☎ 01 45 51 06 04

La Fontaine de Mars

129, Rue Saint-Dominique, 75007
☎ 01 47 05 46 44
www.fontainedemars.com

Un Jour de Fleurs

22, Rue Jean Nicot, 75007
☎ 01 45 50 43 54
www.ericchauvin.fr

Marché Saxe-Breteuil

Ave de Saxe, between Place de
Breteuil and Ave de Ségur, 75007
Thurs 8 a.m. to 1.30 p.m.
Sat 8 a.m. to 2 p.m.

Marie-Anne Cantin

12, Rue du Champ de Mars,
75007
☎ 01 45 50 43 94
www.cantin.fr

Museé de l'Armée

Hôtel des Invalides, 75007
Place des Invalides
☎ 01 45 55 37 70
www.invalides.org

Musée Rodin

Hôtel Biron
79, Rue de Varenne, 75007
☎ 01 44 18 61 10
www.musee-rodin.fr

ADDRESSES

La Pagode

57 bis, Rue de Babylone, 75007
☎ 01 45 55 48 48
www.etoile.cinemas.com/
pagode/salles

Au Petit Sud-Ouest

46, Avenue de la Bourdonnais,
75007
☎ 01 45 55 59 59
www.au-petit-sud-ouest.fr

Rue Cler Market Street

Between Rue de Grenelle and
Avenue de la Motte Picquet,
75007
Tues to Sat 10 a.m. to 6 p.m.;
Sun a.m.

Stéphane Secco

20, Rue Jean Nicot
☎ 01 43 17 35 20

Le Violon d'Ingres

135, Rue Saint-Dominique, 75007
☎ 01 45 55 15 05
www.maisonconstant.com

CHAPTER EIGHT

Mille-Feuille à la MINUTE

◆◆◆

3e

RUE REAUMUR

Goumanyat et
son Royaume

Jacques Genin

Derrière

Café Charlot

Le Marché
des Enfants
Rouges

Bob's
kitchen

RUE DE TURENNE

Pain
de Sucre

Rose Bakery

Merc

Hôtel du
Petit Moulin

Matières
à Réflexion

Abou
d'Abi Bazar

RUE SAINT - ANTOINE

4e

Place des
Voges

N

I have always loved the Marais district with its exhilarating bouquet of flavours – a potent infusion of art, culture, history, fashion and style. Sunday afternoons here were always a treat, peering into secret courtyards, shopping at one-off boutiques and tucking into a soft, warm falafel. In recent years, however, the strong, seductive brew that I remember has been watered down. Generic fashion chains and Starbucks have moved in, and while you can still get a great falafel, the traditional Jewish food shops on the once-quaint Rue de Rosiers are gradually being replaced by big-name designer stores. Behind the commercial buzz, you can feel a soft melancholy in the *Pletzl* (Yiddish for 'the little place' and the unofficial name for the Parisian Jewish quarter) as its history is slowly scrubbed away. The tide of gentrification has seen rents and real estate prices soar and have put many premises beyond the reach of the local community.

When the Marais (the 4th) started to lose its free-spirited soul and the edge that everyone loved, the *bobos* (bourgeois bohemians) looked north. Consequently, in recent years, the Upper Marais neighbourhood in the 3rd, also known as *Marais Nord, Le Haut Marais* and NOMA (North of Marais), has become one of the fastest moving and most exciting districts in the city. Avant-garde artisans, hip hotels, young fashion designers and indie boutiques have brought a raw, creative energy and optimism to the medieval streets. Still fresh, laid-back and authentic, this hipster village is not just a hotbed of experimental art and fashion. Here, the adventurous gastronome will find affordable, casual restaurants and cafés with interesting food choices. Poked away down back streets, passionate bakers are creating new twists on traditional fare, and many addresses in the area are serious about organic, locally sourced products. The Marais district has a long association with food. During the Middle Ages the area was a labyrinth of market gardens and fruit orchards that were gradually squashed under the weight of splendid mansions as the aristocracy moved in.

The Upper Marais neighbourhood is liveliest on the weekends, when casually dressed residents emerge for a late brunch and hang out on the café terraces, but compared with a Sunday in the heart of the Marais, when the crowded streets are closed to motorised traffic, it's still refreshingly low-key. You may have to walk a little further to join the good-address dots, but that only sharpens the appetite! Alternatively, grab a *Vélib* (rented bicycle) to get around, and feel like a local.

⟨⟨⟨⟩⟩

It's 10 a.m. and I head straight for Pain de Sucre near the Centre Georges Pompidou. The dreamy little pâtisserie is just opening its doors when I arrive and I drool over the giant marshmallows lined up in the window: soft and squishy cubes of colour beckoning from oversized glass buckets. They come in an exotic range of flavours, from golden saffron and delicately perfumed orange flower to the striped vanilla, olive oil and rose water, but these *guimauves* are only the wobbly tip of the treats found inside.

Pain de Sucre

Eye-catching tartlets are filled with pools of pale lemon, or piled high with tiny *fraises des bois* (strawberries of the woods),

or studded with summer raspberries. There are breathtaking
gateaux and arresting tarts fashioned in large, attractive squares,
like pretty patchwork quilts. While tradi-
tional recipes are respected, pastries are
innovative with new colours, textures
and flavours. The *pirouette framboise*, for
example, is an appealing tart filled with
almond, pistachio and lime cream and
patterned with raspberries. Then there
are the glistening *baba au rhums*. Each
drunken cake is stabbed through the
heart with an extra little pipette of rum,

Pain de Sucre

allowing tasters to choose their own strength of booze. The
collection of these original and clever pastries changes regularly
so a visit will always bring an element of surprise. On weekends,
there is an even greater range. Conveniently, it happens to be
time for morning tea, and also conveniently, there are a few little
tables out the front. I choose a pastry, sip my coffee and watch
the Marais wake up.

In the shop next door is Pain de Sucre's boulangerie. This
set-up allows owners and married couple Nathalie Robert and
Didier Mathray to access both stores from their kitchens at
the back. The talented pair met when they worked for Pierre
Gagnaire as pastry chefs in his three-Michelin-star restaurant.
Blossoms of pale pink peonies sit on the counter and behind are
traditional baguettes and dense, rustic loaves of rye and cereal
breads in whimsical wire baskets. I ask Nathalie what is popular
in the boulangerie. 'The Pain de Sel,' she says. 'It's buckwheat
pâte brisée with *foie gras* inside.' It looks deceptively like an Aussie
meat pie. The *chausson feuilleté aux pommes* is also very popular:
sweet apple wrapped in a flute of sticky pastry that is perfect for
munching on the street. Another irresistible little snack is the

pain roulé, a soft scroll of bread filled with spinach, bacon and cheese.

Pain de Sucre is an ideal place to pick up picnic fare. There are sandwiches, terrines to slather on that crusty bread, and little Girandole tarts. I watch as the assistant lowers one into a smart red cardboard purse to take away; the sturdy wall of pastry holds a confit of onions and cherry tomatoes in a golden egg mixture. Perky sprigs of rosemary are planted on top. Nathalie tells me they also do *grandmère* desserts, traditional old-fashioned offerings such as endearing glass pots filled with rice pudding with vanilla from Madagascar, rhubarb with layers of lemon cream and crumble, or whole cherries with crunchy dark-chocolate mousse.

Girandole tart,
Pain de Sucre

Content, I wander off down Rue des Francs Bourgeois, the fence-line that divides the 3rd and 4th arrondissements, and one of the major shopping streets in the area. Boutiques are slowly opening up. They tend to open quite late throughout this entire area, sometimes not until midday, so best not to plan an early-morning shopping spree.

I turn left on to Rue Elzévir and slip into the Musée Cognacq-Jay. A visit to this delightful and intimate museum can be compared to sneaking around an aristocratic French home in the eighteenth century. I reacquaint myself with the sumptuous collection of furniture and artwork amassed by the founder of La Samaritaine department store and his wife in the 1900s. In under an hour, I emerge back out into the twenty–first century and, one street over, pass another impressive museum, the Musée National Picasso, set in a gracious seventeenth-century mansion. Works by the great Spanish artist reflect all phases of his creative career and include paintings, drawings, photographs, illustrations and sculptures. The museum is currently being given a fresh lick of paint. Newly renovated, modernised and expanded, the exhibition space promises to be vastly improved, with triple the area dedicated to collections. Five hundred of Picasso's works will be displayed throughout four levels.

From here, I start to meander up Rue Vieille du Temple but I don't get far. Across the road from the back of the museum,  I stop to rummage through a vintage wardrobe brimming with Hermès, Chanel, Gucci, Dior, Yves Saint Laurent and Louis Vuitton. 25 Janvier is just the place for luxury cast-offs, and there is everything from dresses and shoes to purses, scarves and jewellery.

If you want to sample a crêpe the way it should be, a few doors up is Breizh Café. *Breizh* is the Breton word for Brittany, the birthplace of the crêpe, and Breton Bertrand Larcher has managed to whisk the oft-mistreated crêpe back to its true roots, respecting tradition while simultaneously tossing it into a new century. There are stacks of choices of *galettes de blé noir* (savoury crêpes made from buckwheat flour), paper-thin with their crisp lacy edges folded into big square envelopes. It's hard enough just to choose between melted gruyère cheese topped with a rosette of *jambon cru de Savoie*, and smoked herring, salmon roe, potato, and farmhouse crème fraîche. Then there are the tender *crêpes de froment* (made from wheat flour) for a sweet pick-me-up at any time of the day. Fancy a crêpe drizzled with home-made salted-butter caramel sauce? You can dither over whether you want it pure and natural or with variations such as cream and a scoop of ginger ice cream, or perhaps with apples and vanilla ice cream. Alternatively, there's dark and decadent Valrhona chocolate sauce, with dark chocolate ice cream.

What sets these authentic Breton pancakes apart is that they

are produced with top-notch, organic ingredients. Premium produce ranges from the finest buckwheat flour to free-range eggs, artisan ham and the famous Bordier butter from Brittany. (Also available in pats 'to go', along with jars of salted caramel.) A visit also provides an opportunity to sample *lait ribot* – French buttermilk, Breizh Cola and Breton beer, or choose from an impressive list of sparkling ciders. This tiny, hectic spot in le Marais Nord has a loyal following. At peak times, reservations are a must.

A little further up 1 stop to browse in Abou d'Abi Bazar, a beautiful shop with a great selection of contemporary women's fashion, accessories and jewellery with a feminine touch. A beacon in the area, the collection comprises *coups de cœur* (personal favourites and love-at-first-sight pieces) from more than seventy selected designers. Many of the items are from French designers, ranging from talented newcomers to more established names. The scramble of surrounding streets has seen dozens of designer boutiques opening up in recent years and if your mission is to shop for one-off fashion and accessories, you could poke around this area – the very heart of the trendy Haut Marais – all afternoon.

'Seventeen ambiences corresponding to each of the seventeen rooms, like seventeen ways of experiencing the Haut-Marais.'

CHRISTIAN LACROIX
on 'Hôtel du Petit Moulin'

On the edgy Rue de Poitou is the Hôtel du Petit Moulin, a great place to stay to experience the upper Marais. Food lovers will delight in the history of this luxury boutique hotel. Designed by one of France's fashion greats, Christian Lacroix, it is housed in a very old bakery, dating back to Henri IV. Local legend has it that Victor Hugo used to buy his bread here. The nineteenth-century façade is graced with lovely murals and a boulangerie sign over the door. The hotel is flamboyantly renovated so that each room

Hôtel du Petit
Moulin

has a different décor, and it's a favourite during fashion week.

One more stop before a late lunch. Also on Rue de Poitou is the fabulous Matières à réflexion. Laetitia Azpiroz and Cyrille Railliet recycle worn-out leather jackets into vintage designer bags in their Paris studio. Old pieces are reworked into more than forty styles for both men and women, and finished with antique chains and clasps. They range from classic and Art Deco styles to men's messenger bags and wallets. Each bag is unique and made from one garment, with the original detail kept. If you can squeeze that old leather jacket into your suitcase, you can select a design and have it made into a new bag. There are also canvas bags made from army pants, a great selection of shoes, scarves and hats for both men and women, and jewellery made by local designers.

It's just around the corner that I am meeting Clotilde Dusoulier at Rose Bakery. This delightful Parisian woman is the author of *Clotilde's Edible Adventures in Paris*, which divulges her favourite restaurants and food shops; the cookbook *Chocolate & Zucchini*; and the popular blog of the same name. Rose Bakery is one of Clotilde's favourite spots in the quarter.

I walk through the long, narrow café past a counter bursting with bright vegetables, wholesome homemade salads and savoury tarts. Ingredients are mostly local and organic. Today, it's just what I need – a reviving, tasty lunch packed with health and flavour. Organic goods in France are referred to as *produits bios* and as Clotilde and I chat over freshly made apple, carrot and ginger juice, she confirms that grains and fresh *bio* products are growing in popularity with French consumers, and becoming more readily available. On the lunch menu there's a nourishing celeriac and chestnut soup, risotto, gourmet pizzettes, a savoury tart with salad, and Clotilde's favourite, *une assiette de legumes*. I follow her lead and tuck into a healthful and interesting array of grain- and vegetable-based salads, served in a rustic pottery dish. The high-quality bread is from Poujauran, one of the most

respected bakers in town, and cheese is from Neal's Yard Dairy in London.

Created by Rose, an Englishwoman, and her French husband, Jean-Charles, there is an English influence in the homey pastries, with moist and chunky cakes, shortbread, scones and cheesecake. On the lunch menu is a fruit crumble *du jour* with *crème anglaise*. The couple formerly ran a gourmet food store in London and this is their second address in Paris, the first being in the hip Rue des Martyrs in the 9th, and more recently, a third in eastern Paris.

Une assiette de legumes

This bobo canteen is my pick for delicious healthy fodder, but if you're looking for an edgier, no-frills version, head to Bob's Kitchen on the Rue des Gravilliers for lunch, another recommendation of Clotilde's, with wooden communal tables, minimalist decor, and a student feel. We're talking lentil soup, bagel sandwiches, veggie stews, quinoa salads and vegan crumbles. Drinks include juice, green smoothies, milkshakes and artisanal beer. The Sunday vegan brunch from 10 a.m. is very popular, when pancakes are also on the menu (and yes, they are even available dairy- and gluten-free). Also on Rue des Gravilliers are two supercool addresses that do Sunday brunch – from midday to 4 pm. Le 404, a Moroccan restaurant, and the eccentric Derrière (meaning behind). Both places have the same owners and share a courtyard that attracts a local crowd. Derrière sits behind the courtyard, hence the name, and masquerades as a quirky apartment inside. The ping-pong table converts to a dining table and you can even eat on the bed. Smokers can slip upstairs into a secret room. Like travelling to the land of Narnia, you enter through a wardrobe.

We spend the afternoon visiting some of Clotilde's favourite stores. As we walk down Rue Bretagne, a street filled with boulangeries and pâtisseries, cheese, meat and fish purveyors, she explains that commercial space in several parts of Paris is becoming so expensive that many small artisan shops have no choice but to move out, as witnessed in the heart of the Marais. Some areas, however, like Rue des Martyrs, have an artisan regulation, where an artisan can only be replaced by another artisan, keeping the authentic fabric and character of these neighbourhood village streets. At the intersection of Rue Charlot is Café Charlot, a *très* popular meeting place for residents of the Haut-Marais. Once a classic old butchery, this hipster address has a great people-watching terrace for a sunny day (sit back and relax, as service can be slow). It's another popular spot for Sunday brunch, and stays open until 2 a.m.

The courtyard of 404 and Derrière

Across from the café is Le Marché des Enfants Rouges, the oldest covered market in Paris, dating to 1615, and a national historic monument. Its name, Market of the Red Children, commemorates the orphanage that previously occupied the site for close to a century, where the children were dressed in red. A much-loved address, it is not so much a remarkable produce market as a quirky and affordable place to eat. On weekends, the market is full of young local couples with kids. Along with the cheese, wine, fruit, fish and flower stalls, there are several ethnic *traiteurs* serving lunch options. What's unique is that the market is dotted with picnic tables where you can sit and eat (with table service), or you can take away. 'Really, it's a kind of food hall,' says Clotilde. The spicy tagines at the Moroccan stand smell divine but Clotilde loves the Japanese Chez Taeko. Here you can opt for dishes such as miso soup, beef sukiyaki with rice, crispy pork tonkatsu, or raw salmon donburi – washed down with a pot of green tea and followed by black sesame ice cream. La Rôtisserie Enfant Rouge serves up crisp Bresse chicken and spit-roasted lamb with spuds. A glass of wine and you're set! Hours are sporadic so check before you go.

We also take a look at Première Pression Provence, a boutique dedicated entirely to one product, the olive oil of Provence.

Première Pression
Provence

Founder Olivier Baussan is committed to authenticity, exactness and purity, and oils are rigorously selected from high-quality micro-producers. Each label shows the name of the grower. As well as supporting and encouraging small domains (the stores are the sole link between producer and consumer), the boutique is strongly committed to ecological solutions and sustainability. Customers are encouraged to return their empty steel cans and refill them from oils on tap, and to custom-blend if they wish. Provence keeps the ancient tradition of producing different oils from green, black and ripe-black olives, and oils are divided into these three categories. As a guide, green fruit is harvested unripe, black fruit is harvested during their transition from unripe to ripe and pressed immediately, and the aged fruit is harvested when completely ripe, and fermented prior to pressing. There are also tasty tapenades and whole olives to sample and purchase.

Our next stop is Popelini, a sparse, intriguing little bakery
with just one counter serving just one thing, *choux à la crème*.
Oui, this sweet spot is exclusively devoted to tiny cream puffs!
The name Popelini comes from the Italian chef who invented
choux pastry in 1540. It's not an address to spend a lot of time
in but rather a place to pop into for a bite-sized snack as you're
passing. These adorable little delicacies are a modern take on
the classic French speciality, have no preservatives or artificial
aromas, and are prepared by hand daily on the premises. Iced
in a rainbow of colours, flavours include pistachio with morello
cherry; rose and raspberry; and milk chocolate with passionfruit.
Each day there is a *choux du jour*, filled with fluffy whipped cream
and fruit in season.

Clotilde steers me across the street and into Cuisine de Bar
& Bakery Poilâne. Recently opened and with third-generation
Apollonia Poilâne at the reins, this Haut-Marais address is the
first branch on the Right Bank of the famous Poilâne bakery (see
page 182) housed in a light, contemporary space. There's the same
small range of beautiful breads and pastries that the primary
store on Rue du Cherche-Midi carries, including that famous
signature loaf, the *miche Poilâne*.

We help ourselves to the basket of
punitions on the counter. These famous
little butter biscuits are crisp and snappy
with fluted edges, and it's hard to eat just
one. As I bite into my second I realise there
is something pure and simple about them

'A little butter
never hurt anyone.'

JULIA CHILD

that adds to their attraction. 'For me,' says Clotilde, 'they are the
taste of childhood.' They remind me of my Scottish grandmother's
homemade shortbread, also the taste of childhood. One taste, two
different memories. They are available for sale in a pretty, pale
green cardboard box printed with 'Poilâne': a perfect foodie gift.

The casual café annex specialises in simple *Poilâne tartines,* made, *bien sûr,* from the famous *miche.* These open-faced sandwiches on toasted bread are created from the finest ingredients and are a good way to sample the bread without investing in a whole

loaf (although you can ask for half, or even a quarter of a loaf, and it does seem to keep forever). For a quick, high-quality, value-for-money lunch, you can't go wrong. There's a variety of delicious toppings, including prawn and avocado, or chicken, anchovies and capers. For a fancy ham and cheese toastie opt for the popular tartine of Saint-Marcellin cheese with Bayonne ham, fresh marjoram and olive oil, melted and crisp from the grill.

Next, we make our way to Merci, the concept store with a big, warm heart. This eclectic emporium is simply stunning; who would have thought it is actually a charity shop! The chic fashion and design mecca was created by Marie-France

Clotilde outside 'Merci'

and Bernard Cohen, founders of the posh French children's label Bonpoint (see page 190). Grateful for their success, after retiring they decided to use their extensive retail experience to create Merci (meaning 'thank you'), as a way of giving back. Proceeds finance an endowment fund that supports educational projects and development in Madagascar. Opened in 2009, Merci is a thought-provoking contrast to the rash of ultra-cool concept stores in the city; here one can truly feel justified in indulging in a shopping spree.

Sunlight streams through the glass roof of the bright, lofty space where three expansive floors hold an interesting and diverse range of products. Beautiful table settings and custom-made furniture are displayed under chandeliers. In various nooks and crannies, you'll find decorative and functional objects for the home, racks of cool designer fashion labels, buttons, ribbons, jewellery, stationery and bed linen. There's also a fragrance laboratory in honour of Marie-France Cohen's late sister, the legendary Annick Goutal (see page 26). A small selection of her gorgeous perfume is sold in flasks at discounted prices and her scented candles are also for sale. For *une petite pause*, there's a cosy café and tea room flanked floor to ceiling with second-hand books, and a *café du cinéma* where classic films are projected on the wall. An organic canteen faces on to a little kitchen garden. As foodies often do, we gravitate to the kitchenware section, where Clotilde picks up a couple of utensils (she's currently working on vegetarian recipes for her new book) before we hurry, with gratitude in our hearts, to our final stop.

'Jacques Genin used to have a private lab and sell to restaurants and hotels,' Clotilde tells me as we walk up Rue de Turenne. 'He opened his pastry shop two or three years ago now, where you can also sit and eat.' This master chocolatier-pâtissier's name seems to be on everyone's lips, not just for his famous caramels and exquisite chocolates, but for possibly the best *mille-feuilles* in town – and arguably the best Paris Brests! Created to mark the first bicycle race between Paris and Brest, the ring shape of this classic pastry represents a bike wheel, and it's the size of a large hamburger. Genin also makes a wicked Saint-Honoré, a selection of tarts from lemon to strawberry to dark chocolate, caramel and chocolate éclairs, and *pâtes de fruits* (fruit jellies). Apparently, even his hot chocolate is to die for!

Mille-feuille à la minute, Jacques Genin

After admiring the pastries and chocolates, I say *au revoir* to Clotilde and settle into the elegant, modern tea room for one of Genin's famous *mille-feuilles montés à la commande* (made to

order), also known around the city as *mille-feuilles à la minute*. They are also available to take away, but with the delicate layering, I'm sure they are best eaten fresh and intact on-site. These traditional French pastries are created by Genin in flavours of chocolate, praline, caramel vanilla, and vanilla-framboise. I sit back and watch pots of tea and pretty tarts arriving on silver trays as my special vanilla-framboise creation is assembled in the lab just up the spiral staircase. As well as Genin's range of pastries on display, he offers diners a chocolate dégustation (a selection of seven Jacques Genin chocolates), and *mini choux* (five little cream puffs).

The small tea selection is from Maison des Trois Thés (www.troisthes.com), a serious tea house in the 5th arrondissement run by Chinese tea master Madame Yu Hui Tseng. One of the world's most renowned tea experts, she offers an exquisite (and pricey) range of nearly 1000 lesser-known and rare teas in her boutique, selecting the leaves in person and overseeing production.

Paris-Brests

Out comes my delicate creation and I take that telling first bite. At once, it is crunchy, creamy and melt-in-your-mouth, the crispiest shards of caramelised *pâte feuilletée* mingling with the not-too-sweet vanilla pastry cream. Then a burst of flavour from the fresh raspberries hidden inside. Divine. The things one has to do in the name of research! I leave with a smile on my face and a bag of those famous caramels – for a foodie gift, of course. If you come on a weekend afternoon, as with most popular tea salons in Paris, be prepared to wait in line for a table.

Just one more stop for the day, the aromatic Goumanyat et Son Royaume. The Thiercelin family has been in the fine food business for seven generations, starting out in Gâtinais near Orléans as makers of vinegar before specialising in saffron production and vanilla trading. The boutique's signature spice is saffron and so enamoured is sixth-generation-owner Jean by these threads of sunshine that he penned the book *Saffron: The Gold of Cuisine*. Perhaps the best spice shop in Paris, Goumanyat supplies saffron, pepper (there's even a Tasmanian one) and other top-grade spices and blends to some of the best chefs in the country. The family also sells a range of fine foods and condiments. Don't miss *le sniff bar*, an array of jars filled with heady spices designed to stir the senses. The highest quality star anise sits beside pale green cardamon pods and *poivres de Damas* – an intoxicating mix of pepper and Iranian rose petals. And then there are the powder-filled drawers in a cornucopia of colours, scents and flavours that invite you into other exotic worlds.

I can't possibly leave without a little saffron. Available in pistils or powders, it is surprisingly well-priced for the most expensive spice in the world. Grown in Iran, bought in France, it will go into a paella I cook in Australia to remind me of this wonderful store in the Haut-Marais. ◇

ADDRESSES

Abou d'Abi Bazar
125, Rue Vieille du Temple,
75003
☎ 01 42 71 13 26
www.aboudabibazar.com

Bob's Kitchen
74, Rue des Gravilliers, 75003
☎ 09 52 55 11 66
www.bobsfoodetc.com

Boutique Merci
111, Boulevard Beaumarchais,
75003
☎ 01 42 77 00 33
www.merci-merci.com

Breizh Café
109, Rue Vieille du Temple,
75003
☎ 01 42 72 13 77
breizhcafe.com

Café Charlot
38, Rue de Bretagne, 75003
☎ 01 44 54 03 30

Chocolaterie Jacques Genin
133, Rue de Turenne, 75003
☎ 01 45 77 29 01

Clotilde Dusoulier's blog
www.chocolateandzucchini.
com

Cuisine de Bar & Bakery Poilâne
☎ 01 44 61 83 39
38, Rue Debelleyme, 75003
www.poilane.fr

Derrière & Le 404
69, Rue des Gravilliers, 75003
Derrière ☎ 01 44 61 91 95
Le 404 ☎ 01 42 74 57 81
www.derriere-resto.com

Goumanyat et Son Royaume
3, Rue Charles-François Dupuis,
75003 (On maps
of Paris, sometimes just
'Rue Dupuis')
☎ 01 44 78 96 74
www.goumanyat.com

Hotel du Petit Moulin
29/31, Rue de Poitou, 75003
☎ 01 42 74 10 10
www.hoteldupetitmoulin.com

Le Marché des Enfants Rouges
39, Rue de Bretagne, 75003
☎ 01 40 11 20 40

Matières à réflexion
19, Rue de Poitou, 75003
☎ 01 42 72 16 31
www.matieresareflexion.com

ADDRESSES

Musée Cognacq-Jay
8, Rue Elzévir, 75003
📞 01 40 27 07 21
www.cognacq-jay.paris.fr

Musée National Picasso
Hôtel Salé
5, Rue de Thorigny, 75003
📞 01 42 71 25 21
www.musee-picasso.fr

Pain de Sucre
14, Rue Rambuteau, 75003
📞 01 45 74 68 92
www.patisseriepaindesucre.com

Popelini
29, Rue Debelleyme, 75003
📞 01 44 61 31 44
www.popelini.com

Première Pression Provence
35, Rue Charlot, 75003
📞 01 57 40 69 58
www.ppprovence.com

Rose Bakery
30, Rue Debelleyme, 75003
📞 01 49 96 54 01

25 Janvier
97, Rue Vieille du Temple, 75003
📞 01 42 71 13 41
www.25janvier.com

CHAPTER NINE

Salted-Butter
CARAMELS

♦♦♦

I alight from the metro and walk through the Palais Royal under the stone arcades, sheltering from the drizzly morning. At the northern end of the gardens I pass a tiny boutique devoted to music boxes and slip out through the narrow passage du Perron. Weaving my way through the crooked Passage des deux Pavillons, I then duck into Bistrot Vivienne, a cosy address at the entrance of **Galerie Vivienne**, for a coffee. This route is under cover for most of the way, so I have only caught a sprinkling of raindrops.

On a rainy day, a ramble through the Right Bank's warren of nineteenth-century covered passageways offers a delightful diversion from traditional indoor attractions, and a taste of old Paris. The passages also reflect a quieter side of the city, giving harried travellers a chance to catch their breath and do some exploring in an inner-city neighbourhood that is surprisingly far from touristy Paris. Coated with a patina of old-world charm, it's a realm of quirky curiosity shops, bric-a-brac and antique stores that offer a unique French shopping experience – especially now, at Christmastime, when the passages are draped with pine garlands and twinkle with tiny lights.

These tall iron and glass-roofed structures with carved woodwork, wrought-iron gas lanterns and mosaic floors became a common feature of the urban scene in nineteenth-century Paris. Once the exclusive domain of the *haute bourgeoisie,* the passages were purpose-built for well-to-do Parisians to stroll through a warm, brightly lit space browsing at luxury boutiques free from rain and mud; they were, in essence, the original shopping malls. Until their creation, promenading was near impossible, and footpaths were a notion of the future. During their heyday in the mid-1800s, around 150 covered passageways ran from Les Halles to the Palais Royal and up to the theatre and shopping districts of the 2nd and 9th arrondissements, enabling pedestrians to traverse these neighbourhoods almost entirely under cover. The arcades also provided an acceptable place for women to wait for carriages and a short cut through city blocks, connecting the 'grand boulevards'. It was a heady era when the grand boulevards were in full swing, the dance halls and theatres were jam-packed, and the city's first restaurants were springing up.

By the end of the nineteenth century, wide boulevards with footpaths took over for promenading, electricity was introduced and department stores evolved. Small shopkeepers were unable to compete and the arcades declined. Today, fewer than twenty remain. The majority are concentrated in the 2nd and 9th and are marked on maps of Paris. While most passages are classical in style, they vary substantially in personality. Some are elegant and polished; others laid-back and scruffy.

I finish my coffee and walk through Galerie Vivienne. It's the most exquisite of the passages, restored to its original splendour. Shafts of light pour through the glass roof and on to the beautiful mosaic-tiled floor. Among the traders are Wolff & Descourtis, draped with chic scarves, and Legrand Filles et Fils, a must-stop address for food and wine lovers. Four generations of the Legrand family have run one of the oldest *épiceries* and wine stores in Paris and the family continues to take pleasure in sourcing wine from rare vintages and small, lesser-known French vineyards, along with Armagnacs, Cognacs and gourmet treats from all corners of France. Behind the nineteenth-century façade, the selection of wine is rigorous, and the family's passion, knowledge and great respect for *terroir* have given them the reputation as one of the best *caves* in the capital.

The universe of Legrand has more recently expanded to include wine paraphernalia (such as Laguiole corkscrews) and a wine bar, where guests can sample regional wines by the glass, paired with a gourmet platter of produce sourced from the best houses. Shame it's so early in the morning, as the Legrand plate tempts me with exceptional *saucisson* from Conquet; terrine and rillettes from one of the outstanding artisan charcuteries in France, Hardouin; and cheese from Quatrehomme (see page 179). A fine reason to return one afternoon. In the grocery, original wooden counters, creaky ladders, and a patterned-tiled floor evoke a real sense of the past. Here, you can still find excellent regional produce and glass jars of old-style French lollies including *Le Coquelicot de Nemours* (poppy drops). These boiled sweets date back to 1850 and are naturally flavoured and coloured with wild red poppies.

'In 1839 it was considered elegant to take a tortoise out walking. This gives us an idea of the tempo of the flânerie in the arcades.'

WALTER BENJAMIN

Perhaps what I love most about this magical area of Paris is the assortment of confectionery shops; it is full of bonbons from a nineteenth-century French childhood with mesmerising names like *Négus de Nevers* and *Bergamote de Nancy*. How can one not be entranced by liquorice whips, *orangettes* and rainbow-striped *berlingots* made from pulled sugar? In a nation famously resistant to change, these *confiseries* are owned by artisan manufacturers with a deep respect for time-honoured traditions, who have preserved the fairytale interiors almost intact, along with bags of old-fashioned flavour.

I turn on to Rue Vivienne and peer through the window of Le Grand Colbert at number two, a listed building with a sumptuous Belle Epoque interior. If you were to go on looks alone, this is the fantasy version of a Paris brasserie. It featured in the 2003 film *Something's Gotta Give* and can also be accessed from Galerie Colbert, a passage resplendent with trompe l'œil marble columns and a magnificent glass dome. Just a slight detour down Rue Colbert is the lovely French bistro Le Mesturet, with an emphasis on fresh food from small producers. Dodging the umbrellas, I continue on and thread through three more connecting passageways.

The well-worn Passage des Panoramas is the first I arrive at and the oldest of the surviving passages, built in 1800. It was also the first in the capital to be illuminated by gaslight. Spectacular revolving panoramas near its entrance also made it unquestionably the most fashionable. Designed by American Robert Fulton and executed by French artist Pierre Prévost, the panoramas (a precursor to the movies) created the illusion of being surrounded by dramatic historical scenes, great European cities or faraway lands. The panoramas changed regularly and pedestrians flocked here for a breathtaking visual treat.

Although the panoramas have long vanished, I stumble upon second-hand bookshops, vintage postcard and stamp collections and the artist's entrance to Théâtre des Variétés, a small theatre house that provided the inspiration and setting for Emile Zola's novel, *Nana*. One address for a special meal is Passage 53. Be sure to reserve weeks ahead to secure a booking in the tiny

Passage Jouffroy,
Le Mesturet,
Passage des
Panoramas

Bois Cirés
FER FORGÉ

SENTEUR POUR LA MAISON

VENTE
À L'ÉTAGE

PANORAMAS
PHILATELIE

IVE GALLERY

Cartes Postales
Lettres...
Patrick Phil...

STELLA
...

Ours de Paris

MARÉCHAL
TIMBRES ET LETTRES
CARTES POSTALES
...

LE MESTURET
NOS FORMULES
LE PETIT MESTURET   23,50€
ENTRÉE + PLAT ou PLAT + DESSERT
LE GRAND MESTURET
ENTRÉE + PLAT + DESSERT   29€

* Harbré de canard
au foie gras, compote
d'oignons aux épices
                        8,60

* Brochette d'onglet de
veau de Corrèze à la
Gentiane, gâteau de
légumes au ras el hanout.
                        14,90

* Île flottante au
caramel d'amande
crème pistache

dining room. The innovative French cuisine is by Shinichi Sato (formerly of Pierre Gagnaire and L'Astrance) and his Japanese team. Pristine ingredients are sourced from the best producers, including star butcher Hugo Desnoyer. Passage 53 earned its first Michelin star in 2010, just a year after opening, and currently has two stars.

Now in the heart of the traditional theatre district, I cross over the bustling Boulevard Montmartre to be swept into the 9th arrondissement and Passage Jouffroy, an eclectic arcade lined with wooden shopfronts. Built in 1847, its original popularity hinged on the fact that it was one of the first heated arcades in the city – and there is still a warm and inviting feel. Here I find the colourful Musée Grévin, the Paris Wax Museum, containing historical French scenes and famous characters from the French Revolution to the present day, along with a trove of unusual and interesting boutiques. My favourite is the antique cane collection at number 34, an eccentric little shop embellished with traditional marionette stage façades.

Directly opposite, at number 29, is Pain d'Epices, an old-fashioned toyshop with miniature treasures for a French-inspired doll's house (think tiny baguettes and tarts, and chandeliers with real light). There are retro French board games and gorgeous old-world toys by Moulin Roty. The store is named after the popular French spice cake, *pain d'épices*, which loosely translates as 'gingerbread' but is more a cross between cake and bread. Due to its hefty dose of honey, this delicious, sticky loaf is often sold at honey vendors.

Comptoir de Famille at number 35 sprawls over two floors and is crammed with French country furniture, quality linen and scented candles.

Up a flight of stairs at the end of the arcade is the quirky Hôtel Chopin. At night, the passage is locked and you need to ring the doorbell at the entry gate to be allowed in, making it possibly the safest budget hotel in the city.

Over Rue de la Grange-Batelière is the third and quietest connecting arcade, Passage Verdeau, selling comic books, vintage cameras and old images.

No sooner have I stepped out into the drizzle than I am stepping back in time again at A la Mère de Famille, the oldest confectionery and chocolate shop in Paris. This enchanting corner store with its bottle-green façade, antique cabinets and star-patterned tiled floor has been in business since 1761, and is a veritable museum piece. Mirrored shelves and marble counters display old-fashioned sweets from all over France, luscious glacé fruits, handmade chocolates and caramels. There are Biscuits Roses de Reims (the French treat is traditionally enjoyed by dunking the pink ladyfinger biscuit in a glass of Champagne), and because it is Christmastime, metre-high candy canes, and *marrons glacés* (candied chestnuts). I feel like a kid in a lolly shop! Purchases

Passage Jouffroy leading to Hôtel Chopin

are still paid for at the vintage glassed-in cashier's booth. Biting into a *calisson d'Aix,* the famous marzipan biscuit from Provence, I can almost hear the clip-clop of carriages, see the gas lamps flickering and imagine nineteenth-century Paris in full swing.

I pop up my umbrella and scurry south along Rue du Faubourg-Montmartre towards Bouillon Chartier. It's time for lunch and to time-travel again. I pass by Rue Cadet – today the little market street is a moving sea of umbrellas – and Rue Richer, home to the famous Folies Bergère music hall.

Chartier does not take reservations but the queue in the courtyard moves quickly. The vast room, listed as an historic monument, is reminiscent of a vintage railway station canteen, complete with an enormous clock on the wall. Raucous and real and full of life, the place is bursting at its wood-panelled seams! Be warned: you do NOT come to Chartier for fine gourmet cuisine. You come to this preserved relic of Belle Epoque, working-class Paris to wallow in Gallic splendour. It's no-fuss, traditional French fare but the drama and nostalgia of the occasion, the theatre of it all, instantly connects you to everyday Paris, both past and present. As the website so eloquently puts it, 'Chartier [. . .] will of course not replace a nice visit to the 7th, but Rue du Faubourg-Montmartre in the 9th is the best place to feel Paris.'

> 'Had I but one penny
> in the world, thou shouldst
> have it for gingerbread.'
>
> WILLIAM SHAKESPEARE,
> *Love's Labour's Lost*

Chartier opened in 1896 as a *bouillon*. This new type of eatery evolved in the nineteenth century thanks to resourceful butchers who turned their meat scraps into nourishing stews and fortifying broths, serving them as a sideline to blue-collar workers at counters in their shop. Business bubbled away and soon the stews and soups began to attract a bourgeois crowd and a clamorous buzz. *Bouillon* takes its name from the soup that formed the basis of these affordable dishes: a mix of meat and vegetables. The Chartier brothers established a chain of *bouillons* in the 1890s but this time-warp address is the only one today that keeps the Chartier name. I am seated at one of the small communal tables.

Next to me is a middle-aged couple, and opposite, a man that Toulouse-Lautrec could have painted, with a face full of character, a tartan jacket and striped shirt. At the adjoining table is a large French family and at this time of the year, the clientele is mostly local, snatching a quick, cheap lunch in the quarter. I watch as the snappy waiters, dressed in long white aprons, black bowties and *les rondins* (black waistcoats with a frightening number of pockets), deliver literally hundreds of meals. The website states that 'fifty million bellies have been satisfied since its creation'. I toss my coat up into one of the elaborate wood and brass racks that run along the top of the tables, and looking higher I see globe chandeliers and a vast skylight. Bevelled mirrors, marble wainscots and a tranquil pastoral mural (which does little to calm the frenetic energy of the place) decorate the walls. The most fascinating antique feature, however, is the square wooden drawers, still numbered, where regulars once kept their own serviettes.

The waiter approaches with a grunted *bonjour*, and hands me a large sheet of paper. Simple offerings include half a dozen snails, country terrine, and *carottes râpées* – only in France could a pile of grated carrot become a classic entrée! I glance at the mains, amongst them *choucroute Alsacienne* and duck confit with parsley potatoes. For dessert: *coupe Mont Blanc*, Peach Melba, profiteroles with warm chocolate sauce – I very much doubt that the menu has changed in decades. Surprisingly, even the prices do not seem to have climbed into the twenty-first century.

Bouillon Chartier

Having resisted another very simple classic entrée the entire time I lived in Paris, I finally surrender and order *œuf dur mayonnaise* (a hard-boiled egg with mayo) along with *poulet frites* and a little carafe of white wine. Realising I am not with Monsieur Toulouse-Lautrec opposite, the frenzied waiter clicks his pen, draws a swift line down the middle of the paper tablecloth and scrawls down our separate orders. A plate of baguette is banged down and the couple's wine comes in an old Pommery bucket. The place is bawdy and fun, and lunch becomes a family affair as we pass the condiments and bread to each other and comment on our dishes. I strike up a conversation with Monsieur Toulouse-Lautrec, a gentle, quietly spoken man. As he politely eats his dessert of *baba au rhum* with lashings of Chantilly cream, he tells me he lives in the quarter. '*Chartier, c'est simple, basique, mais très Parisien,*' he shrugs (Chartier, it's simple, basic, but very Parisian).

That just about sums the place up.

◇◇◇◇◇

After lunch, I head further into the 9th. As well as being the hub of theatre, where artists rubbed shoulders with the aristocracy, this arrondissement was the heart of France's art and antiques market. A short walk away on Rue Drouot, I drift into Paris's central auction house, Hôtel Drouot, for a look. A drab 1980s building that stands out like an Aussie accent, it's open to the public for viewing and sales, and everything from fine art to haute couture gowns go under the hammer. Today, I find one room of samurai swords and Chinese masks, and another with vintage children's tea sets, matchbox toys and an express train with a 'Wagon Restaurant' dining car. Upcoming auctions can be found in the weekly *La Gazette Drouot*, available from kiosk newsstands. In the streets surrounding the auction house there are still coin and stamp collectors, and small art and antique galleries. Rue Laffitte and Rue Peletier were home to a number of famous dealers and galleries, and were the centre of the Parisian market for contemporary art. Claude Monet was born on Rue Laffitte in 1840 and lived here as a young boy. Throughout his life, the loyal epicurean maintained a steady supply of treats from Fouquet, one of the best *confiseries* of the day that opened on Rue Laffitte in 1852. Many of the nineteenth-century chocolates, bonbons and jellies that Monet enjoyed are still available in the old-fashioned sweet shop, handcrafted to the original recipes.

From Hôtel Drouot I meander up the hip Rue des Martyrs, a lively merchant street in the heart of a neighbourhood that's home to a young, creative community and middle-class families attracted to the 9th for its large, spacious apartments, affordable real estate and central location. The bottom of the street is lined with food shops, while the feel changes near the top with its proximity to the red light district of Pigalle.

It's Wednesday, school is out and Käramell is full of children filling bags with mixed lollies from the serve-yourself wooden boxes. The modern lolly shop, in contrast to other *confiseries* in the district, is brimming with bright and unusual Scandinavian sweets, purchased by weight. Lena Rosen's treats are low on sugar, and as well as hard candies, fruit gums and marshmallows, there is a range of salted liquorice and original black Swedish fish (chewy, fish-shaped lollies with a salty flavour – definitely an acquired taste). There are also colourful clogs and intriguing gifts.

Further up is the boulangerie/pâtisserie Arnaud Delmontel where Alsatian *tartes linzers* oozing with raspberry jam vie with mango cheesecakes for attention. A recent addition for the kids of the quarter is the *brins de choc*, a bag of ten biscuit batons dipped in premium chocolate. Arnaud Delmontel is known for his excellent breads as well as pastries, and the star of these is the tall, handsome Renaissance. This traditional baguette, named after the corner building, is a regular annual contender for the Best Baguette in Paris. Delmontel was a pioneer in resurrecting French bread by returning to age-old traditions, and the Renaissance was voted *Meilleure* (best) *Baguette de Paris* in 2007. In March of each year, a panel of food experts gather to choose the city's best baguette. On top of the cash prize and prestige, the baker is given the honour of supplying the official residence of the President, the Elysée Palace, with baguettes for a year.

At the top of the hill, I catch glimpses of Sacré-Cœur over the rooftops, like apparitions from an Utrillo painting. Munching on my pastry from Delmontel, I turn left on to Rue Victor Massé, a street filled with musical instrument shops. It's also home to Le Pantruche, an excellent neighbourhood bistro with a two-course lunch menu for €18. Chef Franck Baranger worked in Christian Constant's kitchens on Rue Saint-Dominique and at Hôtel Le Bristol with Eric Fréchon before opening this simple little spot in bohemian So-Pi (South of Pigalle).

Further on, I peer through the wrought-iron gate of Avenue Frochot. This leafy, gated street is an exclusive residential enclave favoured by the film and fashion world, and was once home to the French writer Alexandre Dumas, who penned *The Three Musketeers*. For contrast, it's only steps from the sex shops of Place Pigalle. Adjacent to the Avenue is Rue Frochot. Like many artists of the time, Edgar Degas took various studios in this neighbourhood, and it was in this street that he painted a number

Käramell (top left and bottom right), Arnaud Delmontel

of his ballet scenes and created his most famous sculpture, *Little Fourteen-Year-Old Dancer.*

My next stop is a tribute to the Romantics, whose haunt was La Nouvelle Athènes – roughly, the area around Saint Georges metro station. The 'new Athens of the nineteenth century' embodied not only the artistic and intellectual spirit of the neighbourhood, but also an entire era of new buildings. With the Industrial Age of the 1820s came economic growth and social change and people flocked to the city. The quiet streets began to flourish with hidden passages, charming courtyards, and mansions of neo-classical design, often influenced by English urban architecture.

Ave Frochot

Brimming with poetry and charm, the Musée de la Vie Romantique (Museum of the Romantics) was built in Italian style as a private mansion in 1830 for the fashionable Dutch portrait painter Ary Scheffer. His Friday-night soirées entertained a glitterati of guests including Delacroix, Rossini, Chopin and the Romantic feminist writer Baronne Dudevant, alias George Sand. It was also here that Scheffer painted his portrait of Charles Dickens, which now hangs in the National Portrait Gallery, London.

The museum is approached via a cobbled lane flanked with ivy and shaded by robinia trees in summer. Pastel-green shutters set the scene for tea under the trees in the peaceful little rose- and lilac-scented garden. The *Salon de Thé* is open mid-April to mid-October and can be accessed without a museum ticket.

Fans of Sand will catch a glimpse of her life and times on

the ground floor. In 1923, her granddaughter bequeathed a large collection of artwork, furniture and keepsakes from the writer's country house to the City of Paris. Amongst the treasures are snuff boxes, lockets, seals with her initials, and plaster casts of Sand's arm and Chopin's hand – one of the few clues here to her eight-year love affair with the famous Romantic composer and pianist. Sand and Chopin lived just a few streets away on Square d'Orléans, on opposite sides of the courtyard. This quiet retreat is modelled on a traditional London square.

Around the corner from the museum is my sweetest and final stop for the day. My experience at L'Etoile d'Or is one I shall fondly remember, like the exquisite salted-butter caramel from Quiberon that the pigtailed owner, Madame Acabo, slipped into my pocket with a smile. These famous caramels, known as CBS (*caramel-beurre-salé*, salted caramel butter), are made by the talented Henri Le Roux in Brittany. From the moment I enter her lolly shop I am charmed, a welcome guest treated like an old friend, and before long, she has given me a delicious tour of France around her glass-fronted shelves. Abaco stocks only the very best, and recipes for many of the traditional French sweets and fine chocolates date back to the 1800s.

Musée de la vie Romantique, Jardin

'I have sweets from all over France – *toute les regions en France*', she exclaims excitedly. One can tell that this is not just a job for Acabo; it is her life, and a sweet fairytale at that. 'Many of my clients are friends,' she says after greeting a couple buying gifts

for Christmas. *'Je les adore.'* I glean sweets from Toulon, Toulouse, Strasbourg and Grenoble. There is apple sugar from Normandy in long batons, beautifully packaged Nougat Fouque from Provence – 'The best nougat in France,' she assures me – and artisan Bernachon chocolate bars from Lyon. L'Etoile d'Or is the sole retailer outside Lyon to purchase these mesmerising tablets of chocolate. There is *jour et nuit*, day and night, a wicked blend of dark and milk chocolate, but being a sucker for salted caramel, I prefer the Kalouga bar: a blend of dark chocolate and thick, oozing caramel. Bernachon is one of few houses in France that make their own couverture, mixing a variety of prestigious cocoa beans to a family recipe.

I pick up a vintage Suchard chocolate tray from the marble counter to gather my purchases on, and spend far more than I intended. One great thing about this storybook place, however, is that although the products are high-end, Acabo is quite happy for customers to choose just a couple of precious chocolates and an eye-catching sweet or two, essentially creating an exceptional bag of mixed lollies to indulge in later during a private moment.

We start talking about the quarter and before I know it, she asks her assistant to mind the shop and incredibly, takes me on a tour of the neighbourhood. At the top of the street, with its red windmill in full view, is the iconic Moulin Rouge. 'There are tons of cinemas and theatres and artist studios around here,' she says as we pass through a nondescript doorway.

RRose Sélavy is everything a creative child (and adult) could wish for, a fabulous hidden gem in the heart of an artistic quarter of Paris. Madame Acabo is talking ten to the dozen as we peek into the maze of rooms full of children on their regular Wednesday off, painting, drawing, making jewellery and turning pots. Girls sew material dolls with their mothers around a big wooden table. There is such an atmosphere of joy in this multi-storey art studio.

L'Etoile d'Or

On the top floor is a kitchen with a large table and funky pink chairs. 'It's not well known,' says our teacher-guide, 'but if you phone ahead we will welcome you for tea or a light lunch – salads, quiches and the like.' Weekend workshops are available.

On our return, I ask Madame Acabo to put together a box of handcrafted chocolates for me to share with my family at Christmastime. All the while, she is chatting away and explaining. If you hope to get out of here in the time it takes to finish a chewy chocolate-and-caramelised-sugar Négus, think again! My chocolates are proudly gift-wrapped in *papier d'Epinal,* sheets of paper printed with vintage comic strips. 'The paper costs a euro a piece,' she says as she wraps my tin of Négus and ties it with a thick red ribbon. Comics have long been a part of French life. Acabo tells me that when she was a child individual squares of these strips were cut out by the nuns and presented to well-behaved children.

I head out the door, dig the CBS out of my pocket, twirl open the cellophane and pop it in my mouth. Instantly, I feel a rush of gustative emotion. I am taken back to my grandmother's country kitchen, to the sweet-smelling Russian toffee that bubbled on her wood-burning stove every year for the church fête. Tin trays would cover her table filled with soft, cooling toffee studded with walnuts straight from the tree and scored into squares of bliss. I hear someone behind me calling '*Madame*' and whirl around to see Denise Acabo scooting down the street after me with my bag of goodies, pigtails and flouncy tartan skirt flying. With my head in the clouds and now with a flash of childhood in my mouth, I had clean forgotten to pick them up! I thank her profusely as she sweetly greets a local passing on the street, and turns back to her shop with a skip in her step. ◊

SALTED-BUTTER CARAMELS

LE MESTURET >>

This bistro off the beaten track is worth a detour, and if you are simply passing, the wine barrels, bunch of flowers and blackboard out the front with its tempting three-course, €29.90 lunch menu, will draw you in. Inside there is a friendly feel and a rustic décor. Le Mesturet is run by the warm and energetic Alain Fontaine who sources his produce from small French farms and wines from small producers. I start with a satisfying terrine of free-range guinea fowl with pickled baby vegetables. By the time I have finished, the place is buzzing and diners are slurping up bowls of authentic *soupe à l'oignon* at the bar. It's rowdy and convivial and packed to the rafters with knowing residents from the quarter, and suits with tickets resto* who come for good, well-priced, regional cuisine. It is very French, but has an English menu. I find the service rather slow but with such an enormous clientele, it's perhaps a consequence of being so popular.

After I finish my rabbit with sweet Jurançon white wine, cumin carrots and grelot onion confit, I sip on my glass of Sancerre and Monsieur Fontaine pulls up a chair. He has a book under his arm and flicks to a definition of Mesturet. Basically, it's old French for 'bad boy'. He explains that dishes are not specifically Basque but his first wife came from the region and he fell in love with the cuisine and wine, so there's a strong influence. 'Sometimes I focus on different regions of France too but we always have une *blanquette de veau*, an eggplant dish, foie gras and a hand-cut steak tartare on the menu,' he says. I had noticed that almost everyone around me was tucking into tartare. 'The fresh meat, from small producers, is finely hand-chopped; we are one of only seven or eight restaurants in Paris now who do this. The beef is mixed with the tartare sauce and served with a shot of cognac to mix in. Tartare used to be made with horse meat, but now it's beef.' It's time for dessert. Two Paris Brests arrive at the next table, but how could I not finish with an almond-flavoured *gâteau basque* from Pâtisserie Paries SAS in Saint-Jean-de-Luz, the traditional dessert of the Basque region? *(Tickets resto: a chequebook of lunch vouchers supplied each month by many French employers to use at restaurants that display a sticker on the door. Their value is co-financed between employer and employee, and is tax deductible for both. There is a voucher for every work day. Not a bad perk.)

**Le Mesturet | 77, Rue de Richelieu, 75002 | ☎ 01 42 97 40 68 |
www.lemesturet.com**

ADDRESSES

NB All passages are closed on Sundays.

Arnaud Delmontel
39, Rue des Martyrs, 75009
📞 01 48 78 29 33
www.arnaud-delmontel.com

Bouillon Chartier
7, Rue du Faubourg-Montmartre, 75009
📞 01 47 70 86 29
www.restaurant-chartier.com

L'Etoile d'Or
30, Rue Pierre Fontaine, 75009
📞 01 48 74 59 55
Unfortunatley L'Etoile d'Or was destroyed in a gas explosion on Valentine's Day 2014 and will be closed until further notice.

Fouquet
36, Rue Laffitte, 75009
📞 01 47 70 85 00
www.fouquet.fr

Galerie Colbert
6, Rue des Petits-Champs, 75002

Galerie Vivienne
6, Rue Vivienne, 75002

Hôtel Chopin
46, Passage Jouffroy, 75009
📞 01 47 70 58 10
www.hotel-chopin.com

Käramell (Söttland)
15, Rue des Martyrs, 75009
📞 01 53 21 91 77
www.karamell.fr

Legrand Filles et Fils
1, Rue de la Banque, 75002
📞 01 42 60 07 12
www.caves-legrand.com

A la Mère de Famille
35, Rue du Faubourg-Montmartre, 75009
📞 01 47 70 83 69
www.lameredefamille.com

Musée Grévin
10, Boulevard Montmartre, 75009
📞 01 47 70 85 05
www.grevin.com

Musée de la Vie Romantique
Hôtel Scheffer-Renan
16, Rue Chaptal, 75009
📞 01 55 31 95 67
www.vie-romantique.paris.fr
Free admission to permanent collection and garden.

Le Pantruche
3, Rue Victor Massé, 75009
📞 01 48 78 55 60
www.lepantruche.com

ADDRESSES

Passage 53
53, Passage des Panoramas, 75002
📞 01 42 33 04 35
www.passage53.com

Passage des Panoramas
11, Boulevard Montmartre, 75002

Passage Jouffroy
12, Boulevard Montmartre, 75009

Passage Verdeau
6, Rue de la Grange-Batelière, 75009

RRose Sélavy
5, Rue Fromentin, 75009
📞 01 40 23 05 95
www.rroseselavy.net

CHAPTER TEN

Terrine Studded
with
PISTACHIOS

◆◆◆

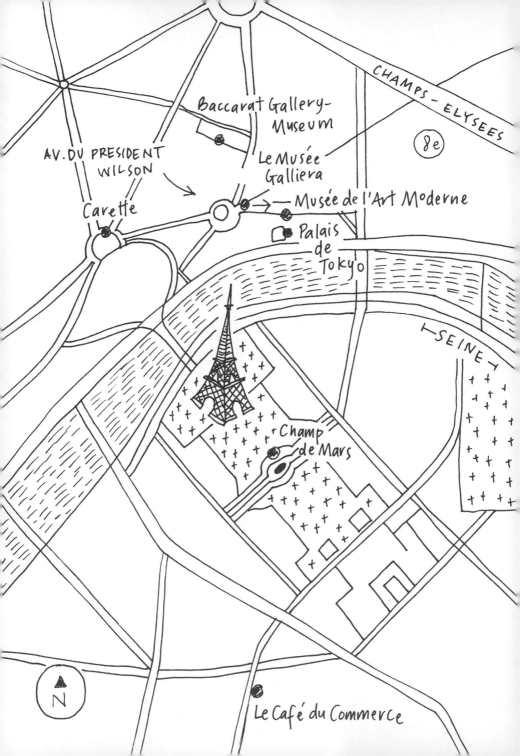

Poke your nose into any corner of Paris and you're bound to find a vibrant open-air food market stocked with mouth-watering treats and tantalising aromas. The French live by the seasons and in a city fiercely passionate about food, *le marché* plays an important role in the daily *art de vivre*. For the food-loving visitor, a market jaunt not only provides a delightful way to sample a bounty of the fresh regional produce packed in the city's hamper, but throws light on the character of a quarter and the rhythm of everyday Parisian life.

Marché Président Wilson

With just one colourful aisle that sweeps you right into the French countryside, the atmospheric Marché Président Wilson is my all-time favourite market and a quintessentially Parisian experience. Nestled in a convenient central location halfway between the Champs-Élysées and the Eiffel Tower, this genteel roving market caters to the well-heeled 16th arrondissement and smart Parisians from just across the river. Avenue du Président Wilson spreads out its sumptuous picnic two mornings a week, under the watchful eye of George Washington on his horse, and showcases the best from the nearby fields, forests and waters. Always busy with an ant-trail of discerning locals, at this market you can be assured of pristine produce.

On a blue-skied Saturday in June I start my day with velvety hot chocolate and a pastry on the terrace of Carette. Not far from the market, on the Place du Trocadéro, it's a good spot for breakfast or morning tea before your visit. With an ambience *très parisienne*, Carette has been an institution on the square since 1927 and remains a favourite tea salon of Parisians who reside in the quarter. Inside it's all gilded mirrors and silver coffee pots, while outside on the rattan chairs you can marvel at the Eiffel Tower. There's an array of wonderful pastries on display and the *éclairs au chocolat* and macarons are especially good. Can't choose between flavours? You can always order a little confetti-coloured plateful. The *salon de thé* is known for its pastries but also serves lunch and dinner, and brunch on Sundays. Although Place du Trocadéro is touristy in peak season, it has a dependable horde of cafés to choose from at any time of the day, all with terraces that provide a memorable peep at the Eiffel Tower.

By the time I step into the market it's crowded and full of life, with vendors shouting out their wares and steam swirling from huge pans of paella. A tiny dog yaps at the butcher, crêpes sizzle on the griddle and spiced Lebanese flatbreads cook on a domed grill. Cradling their baskets, locals banter away as the irresistible aromas of hot rôtisserie chickens and roast potatoes float by, evoking the comforting feel of a home kitchen. The markets are busiest on weekends, when locals come to buy tempting fresh produce to enjoy and cook up with their families and friends, and since our family lived in Paris, there has been a noticeable rise in prepared foods, as well as scrumptious ethnic specialities.

I wander past French country table linen and a fragrant *pâtisserie artisanale* selling rustic cherry tarts. A zealous vendor sharpens his range of Laguiole knives for sale, showing them off on tomatoes. Baskets brim with blushing peaches, fat paint-brushes of white asparagus and dainty posies of violets. Perfume rides the gentle breeze and on this sweet summer day, the array of flowers is simply breathtaking, with hundreds of stems of roses

Marché Président Wilson

stacked sideways into pretty mosaic hedges. Customers choose their blooms, and bouquets are arranged on the spot or while they shop. Most of all, I love the peonies (*les pivoines*), delicate upturned petticoats of blossom in shades of fuchsia pink and swirling strawberries-and-cream.

> 'When one has tasted watermelons one knows what angels eat.'
>
> MARK TWAIN

Further on at the charcuterie, a thick slice of terrine studded with pistachios is being wrapped, and another spiked with cognac. The cheesemonger is cutting a giant wheel of Comté from the Jura Mountains into wedges, alongside ripe artisanal cheeses displayed on little straw mats. Together with heirloom beefsteak tomatoes, bags of cherries, watermelon, and sweet-scented strawberries, they plead to be taken on a picnic. Stacked in crisscrossed towers, I can hear the crackling sound of those dark-crusted baguettes as I picture biting into a piece slathered with goat's cheese.

If you're a curious and inquisitive traveller, a market trip is not only an entertaining outing, but an educational one. It's best to arrive relatively early when the stalls are still bountiful works of art – and none are as dazzling as the fish-mongers. Gazing at the labelled displays, acrobatically arranged on frosty beds of ice, is like taking an enlightening boat ride around the French coast and surrounding waters. Poissonnerie Lorenzo has a part-icularly attractive selection of fish and crustaceans and depending on the time of year, you may find fluted fans of

Coquilles Saint-Jacques from Normandy, wild *palourdes*, the prized cherry-stone clams with a marbled shell, and *moules de bouchot*, superior mussels from the bay of Mont-Saint-Michel. Then there are cockles, whelks and winkles, and coral-coloured *saumon Label Rouge d'Ecosse*. According to the Scottish Salmon Producers' Organisation, 'Scottish salmon was the first fish and first non-French product to be awarded the Label Rouge quality mark, the official endorsement by the French authorities of the superior quality of a food or farmed product.'

When it comes to vegetables, Joël Thiébault is the superstar of the market. In fact, this market gardener extraordinaire is

the Parisian Vegetable King and his stand beams with an abundant variety of beautiful vegetables and herbs all year round. It's difficult to miss the never-ending queue at *Le Maraîcher au Grand Cœur*, where eager shoppers snap up his old-world peas, yellow and purple carrots, and waxy charlotte potatoes. Today, there are nosegays of multi-coloured radishes, flowering oregano and perfumed bunches of orange and lemon thyme, each signposted with an evocative description. A world of tender salad greens is just waiting to be tossed and splashed with vinaigrette.

Always on the look-out for new and rare varieties, this passionate heirloom farmer is dedicated to flavour, seasonality and freshness, and exchanges seeds with producers around the globe. Thiébault grows hundreds of varieties of vegetables on the same land that his family has been turning since the Middle Ages, just a few kilometres (as the pigeon

'Long live the sun which gives
us such beautiful colour.'

_____

PAUL CEZANNE

flies) from the Eiffel Tower. The extensive stand has the feel of a rambling country garden, and discriminating regulars delight in his exotic range of vegetables and heirloom treasures freshly cut, plucked or dug from the earth. Here you can pick and choose, unlike some of the more formal stands, where you will be scolded for touching the merchandise. This direct connection to the source is something that makes shopping here even more special. In fact, some of Paris's best chefs make the pilgrimage in the early mornings for first pick of his exceptional produce for their market-driven menus. In recent years, vegetables have grown in importance, even becoming the stars of the plate, and menus in the city's best restaurants are showered with the bright and unusual, often supplied by Thiébault.

Look beyond the busy stalls and you'll soon realise that Marché Président Wilson is sandwiched between three popular museums. On the southern side of the avenue is the rebel Palais de Tokyo with its avant-garde exhibitions, and the internationally renowned Musée d'Art Moderne. Even if you're not a museum buff I highly recommend integrating a fleeting visit to the Museum of Modern Art into your morning (it opens at 10 a.m.). Access to the permanent collection of twentieth-century art is free, and twenty minutes is all you need to race up the steps and admire two monumental works: Raoul Dufy's breathtaking _The Electricity Fairy_, comprising 250 panels, and Henri Matisse's famous _La Danse_ (and its first unfinished version). Each is located in an enormous, specially designed room. The views across the Seine to the Eiffel Tower from the museum are equally spectacular. Bags and picnic supplies have to be left at the _vestiaire_, however – and on a clear, midsummer day it would indeed be a crime _not_ to gather goodies for a picnic.

On the northern side of the market is the third 'museum in
the sandwich', Le Musée Galliera. Lovers of *la mode* will adore
a visit to this glamorous museum of fashion, located conveniently close to the city's prestigious couture
houses. Set in a sumptuous Italianate
palace built for the Duchesse de Galliera, it
currently warehouses over 100 000 pieces
of clothing and elegant accessories from
the eighteenth century to the present day.
The museum presents temporary exhibitions only, on a specific theme or by a
single couturier, revealing only a glimpse
of its wardrobe-to-die-for at a time. This
rotation is essential to preserve the fragile
collection. Many creations are by grand
couturiers and you never know what you
might see; perhaps the Dior wedding dress
worn by Brigitte Bardot, a classic 1930s

Chanel suit, or a dress donated by Princess Grace of Monaco.

Vélib bikes

Now, where to go for that picnic? Well, if you don't want
to venture far, plonk yourself on a park bench in the fashion
museum's little garden. Access is free to *le jardin* (though not the
museum), and you enter via the Avenue du Président Wilson.
Or just a couple of streets north there's another little park by
another glam little *musée*, the Baccarat Gallery-Museum. Housed
in a former mansion transformed by designer Philippe Starck,
this magical crystal palace is the perfect setting for Baccarat's
headquarters and most beautiful accomplishments. The French
company's international reputation originated from a prestigious
order placed by King Louis XVIII, and royalty and heads of state
steadily succumbed to the charm of Baccarat crystal. Tableware
was fashioned for the Shah of Iran and all the sultans and kings

of the Mediterranean Basin, and throughout the nineteenth century, sumptuous lighting was delivered to the palaces of Northern India, carried across the continent by elephants. Well worth a visit, there are splendid jewels, *arts de la table,* legendary collections and monumental pieces such as the Tsar Nicholas II candelabra. Even *les toilettes* are surprising! The three levels accommodate boutiques, the (pricey) Cristal Room restaurant, and an intriguing gallery-museum where you can find perfume bottles designed for Guerlain and Dior, fragile chalices and a cognac bottle ordered by Prince Rainier of Monaco.

If you don't mind venturing further afield for your picnic, skip back to Place du Trocadéro and hop on the number 30 bus at its terminus at the top of Avenue Kléber. The bus will whizz you around the Arc de Triomphe and drop you off at the marvellous Parc Monceau (see page 40). There is a kiosk where you can buy drinks and ice cream, a playground, and you can even sit on the grass, a rarity in Paris. Public toilets are also scarce in Paris, but you'll find them here. You may prefer to go by Vélib but unless you have a death wish, best to skirt around the Arc.

Alternatively, you could, as I do, simply cross the river to the Champ de Mars and picnic at the foot of the Eiffel Tower. You can sit on the grass here too, although it can be rather trampled in peak season so a rug of sorts is a good idea.

Rue du Commerce

From the Champ de Mars it's just a short walk to Rue du Commerce in the residential 15th, a secret shopping street hidden ridiculously close to the city's principal tourist attraction. The draw is the street's authenticity and village-like atmosphere, and the typical neighbourhood street ends at the steps of the quarter's Catholic church with its tall stone steeple. Leaving the camera-toting crowds behind, here you shop with the locals. There is a good mix of upscale designer boutiques and affordable fashion, with familiar names such as Petit Bateau, Princess Tam Tam, H&M and the wonderful children's store DPAM. The peaceful little park halfway down is a good place to pause, or grab a coffee on the terrace of the corner café that overlooks it.

I take a peek inside Le Café du Commerce. The Art Deco interior of this three-tiered, traditional French brasserie is fabulous, and on warm days, a huge skylight in the roof slides open to let in the fresh air. An address with many lives, it was once a haberdashery, *un bouillon*, and a canteen that fed workers from the Citroën factory and various automobile industries that flourished in the quarter in the 1920s. Run by passionate foodies, there is outstanding beef from the Limousin region served with excellent, homemade chips, and wines from small vineyards. The multigenerational crowd gives the place a warm feel, and it's a good choice for a family lunch. Today, the dessert special is *crème brûlée* with cherries. It's hard to beat the affordable lunch formula displayed on the blackboard outside – a main course and dessert for €15 – but that's for another day. ◊

A pause on the terrace

'Life is just a bowl of cherries.
Don't take it serious;
life's so mysterious.'

GEORGE GERSHWIN

ADDRESSES

Baccarat Gallery-Museum

11, Place des États-Unis, 75116
📞 01 40 22 11 00
www.baccarat.com

Le Café du Commerce

51, Rue du Commerce, 75015
📞 01 45 75 03 27
www.lecafeducommerce.com

Carette

4, Place du Trocadéro, 75016
📞 01 47 27 98 85
www.carette-paris.com
Opens 8 a.m.

Marché Président Wilson

Avenue du Président Wilson
from Place d'Iena to Rue
Debrousse, 75016
Wednesday 8 a.m. to
1.30 p.m.; Saturday 8 a.m.
to 2 p.m.

Musée d'Art Moderne de la Ville de Paris

11, Avenue du Président Wilson,
75116
📞 01 53 67 40 00
www.mam.paris.fr/en

Musée Galliera

10, Avenue Pierre Ier
de Serbie, 75016
📞 01 56 52 86 00
www.galliera.paris.fr

Palais de Tokyo

13, Avenue du Président Wilson,
75016
📞 01 81 97 35 88
www.palaisdetokyo.com

CHAPTER ELEVEN

Confit de CANARD

◆◆◆

SEINE

Le Rideau de Paris

Bonpoint fin de Séries outlet

Deyrolle

L'Atelier de Joël Robuchon Saint Germain

RUE DU BAC

Musée Maillol

Ryst-Dupeyron

Fromagerie Barthélémy

B.D. SAINT-GERMAIN

Du Bout du Monde

Diners en ville

La Pâtisserie des Rêves

Blanc d'Ivoire

Napoleon's Tomb

Les Toiles du Soleil

La Mine d'Argent

Le Bac à Glaces

RUE DE BABYLONE

Poilâne

La Grande Epicerie

7e

6e

Fromagerie Quatrehomme

RUE DE SEVRES

Hôtel La Belle Juliette

Le Jardin du Luxembourg

RUE DU CHERCHE-MIDI

N

L'Académie Américaine de Danse de Paris

Joséphine 'Chez Dumonet'

I am walking up Rue de Sèvres dreaming of crisp-skinned duck when I notice the pungent aroma of cheese in the air. **Quatrehomme** is the culprit. This popular store on a street that neatly slices the 6th from the 7th arrondissement is one of the premier *fromageries* on the Left Bank and not only supplies many of the stylish dinner parties in this part of town but some of the best restaurants in the city. Full of poking, sniffing customers, the bright and busy store is just as I remember it and I find it impossible to pass without craving the incredibly creamy Saint-Marcellin. Quatrehomme stocks around 200 perfectly ripened cheeses and is well known for its Beaufort from the Savoie and aged Comté. In 2000, Marie Quatrehomme was the food trade's first female *Meilleure Ouvrière de France (MOF)*, or 'best artisan in France', a prestigious title awarded to craftspeople in various specialities every four years. Food categories include cheese, chocolate, pastry-making and cooking.

I make a left down Rue Mayer. At the end of the street is Joséphine 'Chez Dumonet'. On the footpath outside, a man is putting the final touches on a grand bouquet of flowers, adding in greenery here and there. The narrow vintage dining room with cracked-tile floor, zinc bar, and white-linen-draped tables makes you feel as if you're walking straight into *la vieille France*. I am ushered to a table by the window while the chef does the rounds, kissing loyal customers from this chic residential quarter. At a whisker past noon, this popular bistro is already filling fast. My jovial waiter, Monsieur Gillotin, delivers an *apéro* of Spanish white wine. 'A gift, Madame,' he says politely. He explains that at this time of the year, December, the clientele is almost all locals, but with the arrival of spring there are more tourists. The man on the footpath staggers in with his enormous creation and places it on the zinc bar. Pedro has been arranging the flowers here for twenty-four years.

I scan the entrées. It's one of those rare menus where everything appeals: morel mushrooms stuffed with veal and served in a rich veal stock, an endive salad with Roquefort, scallops with baby spinach. I take Monsieur Gillotin's suggestion of 'a half serve of artichoke in lemon butter'. A tiny bowl of *potiron*, thick pumpkin soup, is placed before me while I wait, and a large ceramic pot arrives at the adjacent table. I ask the distinguished Frenchman dining with his wife what he has ordered.

Monsieur Gillotin

'*Pot de harengs, salade de pommes de terre tièdes,*' he replies. This help-yourself pot of herrings in oil is accompanied by warm potato salad. After the pot is whisked away to another table, we start chatting. 'We live just across the road and come here regularly. It's always good,' says his wife. 'You should try to come for dinner though, the ambience is even better with candlelight.'

Dining alone has its benefits. You never know whom you might meet or what interesting morsels you might be privy to, and in Paris I rarely feel self-conscious as I would in Australia, because the importance of food eclipses everything. The waiters, who mill about the zinc bar in quiet moments, come up and chat and joke. We talk about food and they recommend restaurants. Soon, the charming couple next to me is joining in. 'Le Dôme,' says the woman, 'on Boulevard du Montparnasse. The *fruits de mer*, the oysters – excellent! It's impeccable every time.' Monsieur Gillotin nods in agreement. The venerable Le Dôme is widely known as one of the best addresses in town for seafood. It's an upscale, classic restaurant, while across the street is the more casual Le Bistrot du Dôme, where simple seafood dishes make up the menu.

The couple tells me about their trip to Australia as a main course of *mille-feuille de pigeon* floats by: layers of potato with boned pigeon in flaky pastry with a rich sauce. Soon, my *confit de canard maison* arrives. The ever-so-crisp duck confit with golden slices of garlicky potato is the dish I have come for. It's often Russian roulette with duck confit. If the skin is crackling crisp and the duck pink and moist, the dish is to die for. If not, it can be one fat disappointment. I take a sip of my house

Chez Dumonet

Bordeaux as Monsieur Gillotin lifts the lid on the Le Creuset casserole the couple has ordered. Immediately the air is swirling with rich, wine-scented sauce. I watch the silky bœuf bourguignon being spooned on to a plate. It is clear I will have to come back.

What you will find at Chez Dumonet is excellent, old-fashioned bistro cooking, a rarity in Paris nowadays, with many of the dishes available in half portions. Nevertheless, I still have to decide between cheese and dessert. I simply cannot fit both in! Reluctantly, I forgo the towering Grand Marnier soufflé and settle for the cheese, the clincher being that it comes from Quatrehomme down the road. As I linger over my generous selection, diners start to leave the restaurant. Then the most extraordinary thing happens, reinforcing my faith in the bond between those who love good food. Having overheard my conversations with the couple next door, more recommendations are offered as patrons stream out the door. 'You must go to Christian Constant's Le Violon d'Ingres, not far from here,' says a well-dressed Parisian. (See page 98.) Everyone nods in agreement. 'We love Terres de Truffes in truffle season, it's near the Madeleine, and for the best view at night, Les Ombres,' offer an elegant couple. From this restaurant on top of the Musée du Quai Branly you peer straight up at the Eiffel Tower.

I say *au revoir* to Monsieur Gillotin and head down Rue du Cherche-Midi. Running from Carrefour de la Croix-Rouge in the heart of Saint-Germain to Place Camille Claudel in the 15th, this discreet, quintessentially Parisian street traces the route of an old Roman road. Embodying Parisian charm, it is filled with classic apartment buildings, florists, clothing and home design stores, and a string of tea salons. It was once famous for its antique shops, and there's still a peppering of them, along with a number of *chercheminippes* (high-end clothing consignment stores).

Next to La Belle Juliette, a glam little boutique hotel in a splendid location, is L'Académie Américaine de Danse de Paris. I heave open the door and excitedly greet Brooke and Vincent, old friends from our Paris days and the owners of this dance school. We chat away and Vincent tells me about Le Petit Olivier (see page 191) just down the street. The ballet school has no café on the premises and Le Petit Olivier has become its *cantine de la danse*.

La Belle Juliette

The long Rue du Cherche-Midi becomes busier as you near the heart of Saint-Germain. Drooling fans lurk outside the famous bakery Poilâne. The store's signature *miche*, a crusty sourdough loaf slashed with a poetic 'P', is still baked in the ancient wood ovens downstairs and the recipe has not changed since

founder Pierre Poilâne opened the bakery in 1932. It would be
a mistake to pass without sampling one of Poilâne's rustic apple
tartlets, a splendid arrangement of golden
pastry and juicy slices of apple. Come early
in the morning if you want to sink your
teeth into one while they are still warm,
or to indulge in a seriously good Poilâne
croissant or flaky *pain au chocolat* – an
unforgettable breakfast that hides a large
bar of quality dark chocolate especially
made by Maison Cluizel in delicious light,
buttery pastry.

Poilâne, rustic
apple tart

My next stop is Le Bon Marché. Chic and elegant, the first
department store in France is a must-visit address. There's
a wonderful selection of *arts de la table* to give those dinner
parties French flair, as well as floors of fashion and accessories
stamped with good taste and classic Parisian style. Regardless,
I head straight for La Grande Epicerie, a feast for the senses that
sprawls like a continuous picnic over the ground floor. A mooch
around this voluptuous food hall is certain to put any gastronome
in a state of bliss. Carrying only the best from France and around
the globe, it offers one-stop gourmet shopping and dream gifts to
stash in your suitcase.

I spy sugar in cubes topped with pale pink rose buds, in
crystals flavoured with *barbe à papa* (fairy floss), and Mariage
Frères tea. France's oldest importer of tea has lured tea lovers
with its heady brews and exotic flavours since 1854 and its stylish
black caddies are always a welcome gift. I move on to the section
devoted to salt, a mineral that seems to be on everyone's lips.
There is the highly prized *fleur de sel de Guérande*, harvested by
hand in Brittany, and a jagged diamond of rose salt extracted
from mines in the heart of the Himalayas. Sold with its very own

grater, it is surely the ultimate foodie gift. It seems that salt (along with pepper) has become the new gold, and you'll find superior varieties sprinkled all over the city, even in the supermarket.

> 'It is a true saying that a man must eat a peck of salt with his friend before he knows him.'
>
> MIGUEL DE CERVANTES, *Don Quixote*

The treats and condiments continue as I weave my way through the hall. It's like a whirlwind tour of France. I pick up a pot of sublime artisan jam from Alsatian pastry chef Christine Ferber (look for the polka-dot caps), a crock of mustard from Edmond Fallot, the last independent mustard mill in Burgundy and fancy Castelas olive oil from Les Baux-de-Provence. There are novelties too, such as Daniel Mercier's edible chocolate teaspoons to plunge into hot drinks or desserts, and tiny tins of Kaviari caviar. I buy one for curiosity's sake and slide back the lid to find a minuscule caviar spoon and a dainty dose of top-quality caviar.

Further in is fine wine and Champagne, and a feast of

artistically displayed fresh foods from glistening fish to fruits, nuts and vegetables. Red partridges sit next to chickens from Landes and plump *poulets de Bresse*. There's a selection of cheeses, gourmet breads and pastries, and in the back corner a pantry of prepared foods to go. *Jambon de parme* and *saucisson des Abruzzes* are picnic-ready, along with classic quiches and containers of bright antipasti. Rustic terrines sit in ceramic dishes waiting to be sliced and slathered on crusty baguette, and there is that divine Jean-Yves Bordier butter from Brittany again.

Just nearby is a delightful secret garden where you can take your picnic. Surrounded by tall stone walls, the Jardin Catherine Labouré at number 29, Rue de Babylone was originally the potager of a convent and is planted with fruit trees and flowers. A shady, grapevine-covered walkway adds to the quiet provincial charm.

The area surrounding Le Bon Marché is a fabulous shopping neighbourhood and most stores in the area, and indeed the city, are open to 7 p.m. I nick down to check out the new Hermès boutique at 17, Rue de Sèvres before spending the rest of the afternoon in and around Rue du Bac. A charming, narrow thoroughfare that curls right through to the Seine, it's one of my very favourite streets in Paris. Bijou little florists overflowing with old-world roses and tulips are poked between fishmongers and delicatessens, while the smell of hot rôtisserie chickens floats down the footpath. Artisan ice creameries, chocolatiers and pâtisseries burst with treats, but the icing on the cake in this village-like street is the abundance of *arts de la table* and home décor boutiques. The question is: how much room is left in that suitcase?

Just a block from Le Bon Marché at Le Bac à Glaces I waver between an apricot and thyme sorbet and a raspberry and rose, before deciding on a lemon and basil cone to zigzag down the street with. All of the artisanal ice creams and sorbets in this tiny shop are made with natural ingredients and fresh seasonal fruit.

I dawdle down the street to the sunny Les Toiles du Soleil and walk right into summer. This 150-year-old French fabric manufacturer produces traditional Catalan canvas in bright woven stripes. Created on old-world looms and famous for its quality and durability, the fabric is made into cheery table linen, canvas sling chairs and their signature espadrilles. It's also available by the metre. Across the road is La Mine d'Argent, where every nook and cranny gleams with silver tea services, knife rests and soup ladles. Most pieces are for the home and table, although

Espadrilles at Les
Toiles du Soleil

a spectacular antique *chariot à pâtisserie* sits proudly, begging to be wheeled to a grand restaurant and laden with pastries. A family-run business for three generations, Daniel Chifman's grandmother opened the boutique in 1930, and today it stocks vintage silver from the nineteenth century and the first half of the twentieth.

I dally down the footpath and into the delightful maze of rooms at Blanc d'Ivoire, set up like a French country home. Defined by natural hues and an elegant mix of antique and modern, the chic homewares collection features painted furniture, lamps, chandeliers, mirrors and *objets de charm*. I'm tempted to move in. Almost next door, Du Bout du Monde mimics a rambling apartment with a contemporary, romantic style. At every turn, I find gorgeous chandeliers, candlesticks, shabby-chic furniture and decorative objects.

Le Bac à Glaces
menu

I criss-cross the street again so as not to miss one of the most delicious addresses in the quarter, La Pâtisserie des Rêves. Each creation is as precious and irresistible as the next in the 'pastry shop of dreams'. Celebrated pastry chef Philippe Conticini adapts the classics and presents his stunning works of art under glass bell domes in his sleek, modern shop that looks like a cross between a science lab and an art gallery. Here you will moan over his lemon meringue pies, *mille-feuilles*, and innovative éclairs slid into sleeping bags of chocolate. Personally, I can't go past the Paris-Brest, shaped like a choux pastry necklace and filled with hazelnut cream and bursts of molten praline. I watch as the inventive creation is placed in a red pyramid-shaped box with a long, looped ribbon, and swing it happily on my finger as I walk out the door.

On the corner of Rue de Varenne is Dîners en Ville. One of the loveliest tableware stores in the city specialises in French tablecloths, cutlery and glassware as well as decorative items for the home. The warmth of the exterior, dipped in claret red and gold, is a delicious entrée to the colourful treasures displayed inside, where an eclectic style and harmonious balance of old and new give a bewitching charm to the richly dressed tables. The owner, Countess Blandine de Mandat Grancey, stocks a kaleidoscopic array of Biot country-style glasses handcrafted in Provence and exquisite cutlery from the region of Thiers, the home of French cutlery and kitchen knives since the Middle Ages. Lampshades come from the countryside near Bordeaux and there is an array of jewel-coloured Beauvillé tablecloths in sumptuous designs. Manufactured in Alsace since the 1700s in a region famous for its textile industry and fabric printing, they make an enduring souvenir of France.

For a break from shopping, you could slip into the Musée Maillol just around the corner on Rue de Grenelle, a lovely small museum dedicated to the work of sculptor Aristide Maillol (1861–1944). Or you could, as I do, squeeze into a smelly little cheese shop a tad further down Rue de Grenelle. Barthélémy is another of the Left Bank's premier *fromageries* and stocks

Diners en Ville

a staggering selection of cheese from all over France, including the finest raw milk Camembert and Brie, Vacherin Mont d'Or in winter and chèvre in spring. Continue along Rue de Grenelle over Boulevard Raspail if you can't resist dipping your toe into a pool of luxury shoe stores, from fantasy creations to hot-off-the-runway heels.

Back on Rue du Bac, don't miss Ryst-Dupeyron, a welcoming, family-owned store that specialises in fine wine, port, Scotch whisky, Champagne and Monsieur Ryst's superb collection of vintage Armagnac, dating to 1868. Inside, it's all old wood and creaking crates of Bordeaux, many of which are from the store's own vineyards. A polished oak table set with bottles and glasses is ready for tasting (purchases can be delivered to your hotel). Labels with personalised greetings can be created on the spot and attached to a special bottle from a chosen year – an ideal birthday or anniversary gift.

Barthélémy,
Ryst-Dupeyron

A little further on is Chocolat Chapon, the sweetest old-world chocolate shop, which has won a sack of awards for its handmade chocolates, and also boasts a wicked chocolate mousse bar (see Chocolate Walk for more info, page 49). It may well be easier to take home a memento from Chapon than Deyrolle. I climb the stairs of this fantastical taxidermy store to find an exotic menagerie of peacocks and polar bears, elephants, tigers and crocodiles. I look up to soaring eagles and tawny owls with wide eyes. If you fancy a stuffed giraffe to grace your living room – a zebra or panther perhaps – this is your place. The four stately salons with high ceilings and grand chandeliers house an eccentric zoo of creatures that could belong in Noah's ark. The back room is dedicated to butterflies, flying insects and beetles. Kids just love it! The store was severely damaged by fire in 2008 but one would never know. More recently, it was a marvellous backdrop for a scene in Woody Allen's *Midnight in Paris*.

On the corner of Rue Montalembert is Joël Robuchon's landmark restaurant L'Atelier de Joël Robuchon Saint-Germain. A decade after opening, this two-Michelin-star address continues to woo with its relaxed brand of fine dining. It's all sleek red and black, and diners can pull up a comfortable stool at the counter and watch the talented young chefs in the open kitchen. With a range of small dishes available, the innovative concept is a fun and delicious way to sample gastronomic French cuisine, far from the stuffy tables of Paris. This dynamic French chef's newest addition to the Paris scene is L'Atelier de Joël Robuchon Etoile on the Champs-Elysées.

A little further up is Le Rideau de Paris, a linen closet stuffed with Provençal and printed *boutis* (quilts), cushions and curtain fabrics, but if you have a little cherub to spoil, scoot around the corner to Rue de l'Université. At Bonpoint Fin de Séries Outlet, you will bump into the local *mamans* who sneak into this treasured address to snap up pretty party dresses and classic coats at 30 per cent reductions. Clothing is from the previous season's collection of this deliciously French brand, and caters for children from newborns to eleven-year-olds. For more good French taste visit the other Bonpoint stores strewn like confetti along this street: 65 (shoes), 67 (children, babies), 86 (boys, mother and daughter).

Blooms outside Au Nom de la Rose florist, Rue du Bac

Not far from the river, giant round boules beckon from the

window at Maison Kayser. Inside are *tartines* and sandwiches, Kayser's popular wholewheat baguettes, and fragrant fig bread.

The celebrated master baker Eric Kayser has stores in a number of locations around the city and is renowned for his excellent, traditional breads. What makes them so good is that he uses a natural sourdough liquid starter. He also excels at pastries and among his plentiful sweet delights are white chocolate-chip brioches and scrumptious apricot and pistachio tarts.

> 'Life itself is the proper binge.'
>
> JULIA CHILD

With the sun dancing on the river Seine, I decide to walk along its banks, through the islands and across the bridges back to the Marais. Perhaps I shouldn't have bought so many souvenirs of Paris. With all these bags I can't possibly swing the box from La Pâtisserie des Rêves on my finger all the way back to the apartment. Besides, the Paris-Brest will probably be a mess by then. As far as I can see, there is only one thing to do . . . ◊

LE PETIT OLIVIER

Dishes are simple, and in this expensive part of town, lunch is very affordable, with menus starting from €10. 'It's an original and unique place – best value in the city,' says Vincent. 'Generally, there are three *plats* to choose from and wines come direct from the vigneron; for instance, a Saint-Emilion Grand Cru 2006 for €25.' Sounds just the place for starving artists!

Like the restaurant, the owner Laurent De Winter is a bit of a character. 'He is incredibly knowledgeable about music. His partner is the well-respected pianist Elena Rozanova. Classical music and opera are always being played in the dining room,' says Vincent. 'It's Violette Verdy's *cantine* when she's in Paris and teaching at the dance school.' (One of the premier ballerinas of the 20th century, Verdy danced in several of the world's foremost companies and was a principal dancer with the New York City Ballet for many years.)

Le Petit Olivier | 82, Rue du Cherche-Midi, 75006 | ☎ 01 77 16 68 74

ADDRESSES

L'Académie Américaine de Danse de Paris
100, Rue du Cherche-Midi, 75006
☎ 01 47 34 36 22
us.aadp-fr.org

L'Atelier de Joël Robuchon Saint-Germain
5, Rue Montalembert, 75007
☎ 01 42 22 56 56
www.joel-robuchon.com

Le Bac à Glaces
109, Rue du Bac, 75007
☎ 01 45 48 87 65

Le Bistrot du Dôme
1, Rue Delambre, 75014
☎ 01 43 35 32 00

Blanc d'Ivoire
104, Rue du Bac, 75007
☎ 01 45 44 41 17
www.petitblancdivoire.fr

Bonpoint Fin de Séries Outlet
42, Rue de l'Université, 75007
☎ 01 40 20 10 55
www.bonpoint.com

Du Bout du Monde
100, Rue du Bac, 75007
☎ 01 45 44 22 38
www.duboutdumonde.com

Deyrolle
46, Rue du Bac, 75007
☎ 01 42 22 30 07
www.deyrolle.fr

Dîners en Ville
27, Rue de Varenne (Corner Rue du Bac), 75007
☎ 01 42 22 78 33
Unfortuately this shop has now closed.

Le Dôme
108, Boulevard du Montparnasse, 75014
☎ 01 43 35 25 81

Fromagerie Barthélémy
51, Rue de Grenelle, 75007
☎ 01 42 22 82 24

Fromagerie Quatrehomme
62, Rue de Sèvres, 75007
☎ 01 47 34 33 45

La Grande Epicerie
38, Rue de Sèvres, 75007
☎ 01 44 39 81 00
www.lagrandeepicerie.fr
www.lebonmarche.fr

Hôtel La Belle Juliette
92, Rue du Cherche-Midi, 75006
☎ 01 42 22 97 40
www.hotel-belle-juliette-paris.com

ADDRESSES

Joséphine 'Chez Dumonet'
117, Rue du Cherche-Midi, 75006
📞 01 45 48 52 40

Maison Kayser
18, Rue du Bac, 75007
📞 01 42 61 27 63
www.erickayser.com

La Mine d'Argent
108, Rue du Bac, 75007
📞 01 45 48 70 68

Le Musée Maillol
61, Rue de Grenelle, 75007
📞 01 42 22 59 58
www.museemaillol.com

Les Ombres
Musée de Quai Branly
27, Quai Branly, 75007
📞 01 47 53 68 00
www.lesombres-restaurant.com

La Pâtisserie des Rêves
93, Rue du Bac, 75007
📞 01 42 84 00 82
www.lapatisseriedesreves.com

Poilâne
8, Rue du Cherche-Midi, 75006
📞 01 45 48 42 59
www.poilane.fr

Le Rideau de Paris
32, Rue du Bac, 75007
📞 01 42 61 18 56

Ryst-Dupeyron
79, Rue du Bac, 75007
📞 01 45 48 80 93
www.vintageandco.com

Terres de Truffes
21, Rue Vignon, 75008
📞 01 53 43 80 44
www.terresdetruffes.com

Les Toiles du Soleil
101, Rue du Bac, 75007
📞 01 46 33 00 16
www.toiles-du-soleil.com

CHAPTER TWELVE

The King's
VEGETABLES

♦♦♦

Musée Lambinet

Trianon
Palace
Versailles

La Véranda

BD. DE LA REINE

RUE DE LA PAROISSE

Marché
Notre-Dame

L'Atelier
Cuisine de Patrici

Palace of
Versailles

VERSAILLES

Le Potager du Roi

N

We are flying down the freeway towards Versailles in a vintage Peugeot 403. I feel as if I'm in an old movie. The gregarious Sébastien is at the wheel, telling me about the upcoming masked ball at the *orangerie* in the Palace of Versailles. Dressed as courtesans and dukes, privileged revellers can re-live the decadence of the time and party from midnight to dawn. The conversation bounces around and soon shifts to the candlelight dinners at Vaux-le-Vicomte, the exquisite jewel-box of a castle south-east of Paris. Guests dine on the terrace overlooking thousands of candles in the gardens and tour the interior of the château where more flickering creates an authentic seventeenth-century atmosphere. Sébastien's love for Paris is infectious and my head is exploding with possibilities as we zoom off the autoroute in the 1950s car that was originally his grandfather's.

Sébastien Bazin is founder of Chauffeurs de Maître, a boutique Paris company specialising in chauffeur-driven vehicles. The small, luxurious fleet, driven by a team of courteous bilingual drivers, ranges from beautifully maintained executive sedans to a Rolls-Royce and Citroën 2CV. The company offers service *sur mesure*, a tailor-made service created according to clients' needs and desires. That may be a special event like a wedding or honeymoon, a shopping spree in exclusive Paris neighbourhoods, a simple airport pick-up or an extended jaunt to a major wine or gastronomic region. Should you require luxury hotel and starred-restaurant reservations, or perhaps flowers delivered, there's also a concierge service. A lightning tour of Paris last night on the back of Sébastien's scooter reveals a born and bred Parisian who knows his city well and eats out often – a bonus for clients wanting insider recommendations.

By the time we pull up in the large town of Versailles, I not only have a yearning to buy a vintage car, I have a page full of Paris addresses. Highlighted are two of Sébastien's favourite traditional French bistros: Chez Paul on the hip Rue de Charonne, and Chez Denise in the Les Halles district, where, from all accounts, it's best to starve yourself well beforehand. I say goodbye to Sébastien, draw a line under Paris and turn the page.

Originally a hunting lodge built by Louis XIII in 1624, the Palace of Versailles was the royal residence for a little more than a century, when the French Revolution of 1789 put an end to aristocratic extravagance. Still bathed in splendour, the château and gardens are undisputedly the top attractions in Versailles. Today, however, it is the town itself I have come to see. Although it offers numerous historical, architectural and culinary treasures, visitors often overlook the former royal city, but as an adjunct to the palace or an alternative day trip, this traditional French town merits a visit in its own right. Elegant and relaxed, with oodles of green space, it offers respite from the crowds and pomp, and a deliciously different taste of Versailles.

I start with a swan around the Notre-Dame quarter. When Versailles was just a swampy little village, Louis XIV created this historic quarter north of the château to serve the purposes of the palace. Its layout was designed to conjure a sumptuous setting and majestic entrance, and magnificent tree-lined avenues that

Chez Denise

once acted as wide, embracing arms for honoured guests still fan out from the palace today.

The quarter was built around three important sites: l'Eglise Notre-Dame (the royal parish church of Versailles), the produce market, and l'Hôtel du Bailliage. Originally constructed to house the judicial district court and basement prison cells, l'Hôtel du Bailliage is now the heart of a quaint network of courtyards and narrow cobbled streets occupied by antique shops. Hours are sporadic but most are open Friday to Sunday. The town has in fact retained a strong tradition of furniture-making and antique shops, a legacy left behind by the skilled artisans and restorers who came to live and work in Versailles. Likewise, there is a culture of gardening, originating from the crop of talented gardeners at the palace, and today, the town is home to the esteemed Ecole Nationale Supérieure du Paysage, the National School of Landscape Architecture. This culture filters through to beautiful fruit and vegetables. Apparently, Louis XIV loved vegetables so much that he requested them with every meal, and glasshouses were heated so that the king could eat green peas in December.

L'Eglise Notre-Dame

The market in the ancient Place du Marché Notre-Dame, the square laid out by the Sun King's architects, is still renowned for its produce today. I follow the converging procession and find myself in one of the most attractive market squares in the region. Stalls are piled high with rustic displays of produce from

'Dreams weigh nothing.'

MARIE ANTOINETTE

the surrounding area, locals are chatting away and there is a friendly, country feel. Around the square are four covered market pavilions. These ancient Halles Notre-Dame are each devoted to a type of fresh produce: *Carré à la Farine* (flour products); *Carré à la Viande* (meat); *Carré aux Herbs* (fruit, vegetables and herbs) and *Carré à la Marée* (fish and seafood that arrive fresh every market morning from Brittany and Normandy). The best time to visit is when the outdoor and covered markets are both open, and if you don't mind a bit of a walk, it's the perfect spot to rustle up picnic supplies before a trip to the château; a delicious and affordable alternative to the lunch options within the palace grounds.

Just off the busy market square is Patricia Boussaroque's cheery little cooking school, L'Atelier Cuisine de Patricia. I climb the stairs of an eighteenth-century building and Patricia ushers me into her bright and contemporary kitchen studio. It's a cosy, feel-good place. Over morning coffee and a chat, I discover that this friendly Frenchwoman worked in human resources for two decades before deciding to follow her dream, swapping her corporate suit for an apron and turning her amateur passion for cooking into a career. After graduating with a *Grand Diplôme* from Le Cordon Bleu in Paris, she scouted around and found a space she could transform into a workshop. At this handy location near the market in her hometown, she has shared her love of good food since 2009.

Marché Notre-Dame

Patricia offers a range of reasonably priced courses in classic, contemporary and regional French cuisine. A class might revolve around a menu of seasonal dishes from Normandy or the Pays Basque, or perhaps focus on how to make raspberry and vanilla macarons, tarts or charlottes. The hands-on sessions run with a maximum of eight participants and the full menus finish with lunch. While there are many cooking schools in Paris, some of the more formal classes in established institutions can be rather serious and a little intimidating, especially when you are in holiday mode. Part of the appeal here is a relaxed environment and Patricia's easygoing and flexible approach, which is especially attractive to gourmet travellers looking for an enjoyable outing as a component of a leisurely day in Versailles.

Although dates for her daily classes in French are set well ahead and posted on her website, Patricia is open to arranging private lessons in English on demand, or making a scheduled class private for a small group. However, her half-day *Traditional French Cuisine and Market Tour* in English is tailor-made for tourists passing through. The course starts with a market visit and finishes with lunch. Sometimes Patricia finds that within a group of travelling companions, the women, for example, may want to do a class but their male partners would rather visit the palace or sit and have a drink (*c'est typique!*). Or perhaps some members of a party have previously visited the palace and are looking for an alternative activity.

All this talk of food is making me hungry and I cross the market square and stroll down Boulevard de la Reine with its majestic parade of clipped trees. A little further on is lunch but I can't help pausing to peer through the ornate grille into Musée Lambinet, Versailles' municipal museum. The thirty or so rooms in this graceful private mansion hold a sumptuous collection of eighteenth-century decorative art, and items relating to Versailles' history and the Revolution – including engraved copper plates used in the printing process of the illustrious Toile de Jouy fabric.

Trianon Palace

I stand a little taller as I walk through the gates of the Trianon Palace and into a right royal setting. The luxurious Waldorf-Astoria hotel in a wooded garden bordering the château grounds

has been a posh place to pause for a string of famous guests since 1910, including Colette, Marlene Dietrich, Sarah Bernhardt and Henri Citroën. As everywhere in Versailles, there is astonishing history around every gilted corner. The Treaty of Versailles, the peace treaty between Germany and the Allies, was signed in the ballroom after World War I.

The Trianon underwent a full facelift five years ago, and today it's a polished blend of contemporary luxury and old-world sophistication. I float through the gallery, where light pours through the windows on to the chessboard marble floor. Guests sip tea and nibble on macarons. With a calm, serene atmosphere, the lush garden hideaway is just a short carriage ride from the castle gates, making it an ideal spot for weary château-goers to restore themselves at any time of the day.

The *enfant terrible* of chefs, Scotsman Gordon Ramsay, orchestrates all things culinary here and his contemporary La Véranda restaurant is the setting for a stylish lunch with a modern take on bistro classics. It's also open for breakfast and dinner, and there's a popular Sunday brunch. Request a table on the lovely garden terrace with a backdrop of the Queen's pastures. It is here that I relax over lunch, starting with *foie gras* pressed with smoked haddock and citrus fruit chutney. Next comes a panful of Scottish scallops with a *fricassée* of artichokes and chestnuts, and I finish with the most delectable *Ile Flottante Revisitée* with passionfruit.

Le Potager du Roi

For a special treat or romantic occasion, the two-Michelin-star

Gordon Ramsay au Trianon is the hotel's fine dining restaurant based on Ramsay's London address. Lunch is only available on Fridays and Saturdays but I poke my head in for a look on the way out. The luscious gold room whipped with cream drips

in elegance and refinement. Dishes are French-inspired, and I surf the €160 tasting menu: 'Raviolo of langoustines and lobster, Petrossian caviar and lime consommé; royal pigeon from Bresse roasted and poached, with potato and artichoke *mille-feuille* and pear and cinnamon purée; chilled pineapple lemongrass minestrone flavoured with coconut.'

From the hotel I take a taxi to the King's Kitchen Garden in the ancient Saint-Louis district, the town's other historic quarter. Known as *Le Potager du Roi* in French, the plot is a masterpiece of French garden art. Jean-Baptiste de la Quintinie created the garden between 1678 to 1683 to produce fruit and vegetables for the king's table and developed the culture of fresh fruit and vegetables that remains to this day. Louis XIV entered his paradise through a beautiful gate at the bottom of the garden, one of the few originals that still exist at Versailles.

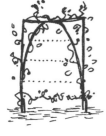

The full-of-beans manager, Monsieur Jacobsohn, takes me for a sunny wander around the potager, pulling weeds and picking samples for me to taste as we go. Retaining its original patch divisions, the nine-hectare garden is fashioned around a central Grand Square and a circular fountain. The Grand Square, composed of sixteen smaller squares, is bordered by striking *espalier* pears, and beyond, there are twelve orchards of fruit trees. Protected behind high walls, they were the king's greatest pride. 'One of the missions of the garden is to preserve historical pruning practices,' says Monsieur Jacobsohn.

At the Carré du Curieux, a square devoted to 'historic aromatic plants, edible flowers, and curious vegetables', Monsieur picks a purple podded pea for me to try before I traipse behind him to the strawberry patch. Here, he plucks three varieties of fruit from the rambling collection of historic and contemporary plants, including a strawberry creation from the 1760s, so I can taste the difference. Nowadays, the National School of Landscape Architecture is responsible for the conservation and management of the gardens, and Monsieur Jacobsohn tells me that they are continually trialling old and new varieties. Taste, uniqueness, patrimonial value and historical interest are all considered in the process.

We trudge past squares of artichokes, peeping stalks of asparagus and a patch of heirloom pear and apple trees, along with peaches and nectarines trained to grow against sun-baked

Le Potager du Roi

walls. More than 30 tonnes of fruit and 20 tonnes of vegetables are produced annually, and if you want to eat like a king, fresh produce is available for sale on Tuesday, Thursday and Saturday mornings. The best time to visit is from June to September. Tours in English are available for groups only but if you grab a garden plan, each patch is sufficiently explained to make an unaccompanied meander worthwhile.

I leave the garden munching on a broad bean. Sébastien is waiting to drive me back to Paris in a shiny black sedan that is fit for a queen. I sink into my leather seat and glide into the city, feeling like royalty. ◊

ADDRESSES

L'Atelier Cuisine de Patricia
Place du Marché Notre-Dame
4, Rue André Chénier, 78000
Versailles
☎ 01 71 42 82 42
www.lateliercuisinedepatricia.
com

Chauffeurs de maître
Sébastien Bazin
☎ 06 60 43 70 39
www.chauffeursdemaitre.com
www.vaux-le-vicomte.com

Chez Paul
13, Rue de Charonne, 75011
☎ 01 4700 3457
www.chezpaul.com

Chez Denise –
La Tour de Montlhéry
5, Rue des Prouvaires, 75001
☎ 01 42 36 21 82

Halles Notre-Dame
(covered markets)
Tuesday to Saturday 7 a.m.
to 7.30 p.m., Sunday 7 a.m.
to 2 p.m.

Marché Notre-Dame (open-air)
Place du Marché Notre-Dame
Tuesday, Friday and Sunday
(largest) from 7 a.m. to
2 p.m.

Musée Lambinet
54, Boulevard de la Reine,
78000 Versailles
☎ 01 39 50 30 32

Office de Tourisme, Versailles
2 bis, Avenue de Paris, 78000
Versailles
☎ 01 39 24 88 88
www.versailles-tourisme.com
Maps and discovery trails
are available here, which
you can also download from the
website.

Le Potager du Roi
10, Rue du Maréchal-Joffre,
78000 Versailles
☎ 01 39 24 62 62
www.potager-du-roi.fr

Trianon Palace Versailles
1, Boulevard de la Reine, 78000
Versailles
☎ 01 30 84 50 00
www.trianonpalace.com

NB: The Palace of Versailles,
Notre-Dame Market, L'Atelier
Cuisine de Patricia and
Le Potager du Roi are all closed
on Mondays.

CHAPTER THIRTEEN

French Onion
SOUP

◆◆◆

Place de
la Bastille

RUE DE CHARENTON

RUE DE LYON

Assaporare

Blé Sucré
La
Gazzetta

Le Square
Trousseau

Le Baron
Rouge

Marché
d'Aligre

A la Biche
au Bois

La commune
Libre d'Aligre

Le Quincy

N

12e

The sun is shining as I skirt around the spokes of Place de la Bastille on this chilly Sunday morning, dodging the scooters and whizzing cars. Once the site of the nation's most notorious prison, the square has long been a symbolic gathering place, where revolutionary battle cries were delivered. Rousing political demonstrations are still held here, and French leftists have converged under the Colonne de Juillet to celebrate their victories as recently as the election of the country's Socialist president, François Hollande. In the centre of the square, the column throws a long morning shadow as I stride past. Balancing on its top, the jubilant winged *génie* of Liberty sparkles in the sun, clutching the torch of freedom. The column was built to commemorate the Parisians who fell in the violent street battles of July 1830 that brought a political voice to the people, and the revolution of 1848.

I turn down Rue du Faubourg Saint-Antoine. Once scented with furniture polish and swirling sawdust, the area was formerly a forest of cabinetmaking and textile workshops, where France's most revered carpenters chipped and chiseled away, creating exquisite furniture for the palaces of Europe. Today, tucked into  a succession of cobbled passageways, the beginning of Rue du Faubourg Saint-Antoine is still dusted with workshops and craft studios. As I rush along, I find it thrilling to think that it was in this historic furniture manufacturing quarter and surrounds that the rumbles of the French Revolution began.

Here in the Aligre quarter, in the garret of the 12th arrondissement, I immediately notice a buoyant energy and more colour in the clothes. The vibrant Marché d'Aligre is the soul and commercial hub of this district in eastern Paris, and up ahead, locals with empty baskets and trolleys are being drawn like supporters to a protest. Three markets in one, it's the only *marché* in Paris that combines an open-air food market, a covered market, and *un marché aux puces,* or flea market. Despite undergoing something of a revival over the past decade, this resolutely working-class neighbourhood is not usually the first port of call for many visitors to the city. Yet, its lively atmosphere, coupled with an interesting mix of food and culture brought about by the ethnic diversity of its residents, make it well worth a detour.

On the corner of Rue de Cotte, I push open the door to Le Chat Bossu and find a seat. The comfortable café is full of marketgoers snatching a morning coffee. Here, I am meeting Marion, a Frenchwoman, and Diane, an Aussie from Melbourne who has lived in Paris for twenty years. They have offered to show me around their quarter. Both are members of the Slow Food Movement and are involved in organising local activities, meetings, projects and events for the Bastille branch, the Convivium Paris Bastille. Originating in Italy in 1986, the movement is a crusader for good, clean, fair and traceable food for all, and opposes the homogenisation of taste and culture. Wholesome local food prepared inhouse has long been a French trademark. Proud traditions mean that age-old businesses have unwittingly adhered to the slow food philosophy for generations, and many small producers and restaurant owners are fierce supporters of high-quality, traceable food. However, there is also growing concern about the army of restaurants that serve 'industrial fodder', with more and more traditional corner bistros being taken over by chains. Leading French chef, Xavier Denamur, is quoted as saying recently that '[Big food groups] have gobbled up the little independent restaurants to end up serving uniform

Marché d'Aligre;
Diane from Slow
Food, Bastille

Banane
DE GUADELOUPE
& MARTINIQUE

OIE

S.A.R.L. RABIER Fils
45150 CRAVANT
Tél./Fax 02 38 44 52 81

food, produced externally in a laboratory.' It can make it difficult for visitors to Paris to know what the pretty façade of a restaurant may be hiding.

Soon we are sipping coffee and chatting away. Both women are advocates of good food that is also good value, and believe it's possible to eat well in Paris without spending a lot of money. 'It's about knowing where to go,' says Diane. 'There are a number of good places sprinkled about the quarter. You must go to Assaporare Italian restaurant and wine bar for an apéritif,' she says, as Marion writes down addresses for me. 'Order a spritz; it may seem expensive at €12, but the nibbles – they just keep coming out, on the house, and they are amazing!' The list gets longer. Two of their favourite places to eat in the quarter are La Gazzetta, which we will pass on our tour of the market, and Le Quincy, a country auberge with timeless classics and regional specialities from the Berry and Ardèche regions. 'It's well known for its *abats* (offal),' says Marion.

On the same street as Le Quincy is another Parisian favourite, the traditional A la Biche au Bois. Surprisingly, three Parisians I have spoken to on this trip, all from different walks of life, named this as their favourite home-style French bistro in the city. In autumn, you'll find plenty of *gibier* (game), from venison with prunes to wild boar with chestnuts. Whatever the time of year, you'll be treated to excellent country terrines, hearty bistro dishes, including a classic *coq au vin*, a lavish cheese platter, and homemade desserts. It's great value for money, but take note: like Le Quincy, it's open on weekdays only.

We wrap our scarves around our necks and head outside. 'Centuries ago', begins Marion, 'this area lay outside the original city wall and was full of market gardens and vegetables.' (Researching further, I discover it was part of the suburb of Faubourg Saint-Antoine. The Church and Abbey

Saint-Antoine-des-Champs owned a large amount of this land, which ran out to the sprawling woods and castle of Vincennes.)

'Before the French Revolution, horses used to deliver wine and food from the port of Bercy to the market at Les Halles,' continues Marion. 'The Rue du Faubourg Saint-Antoine nearby was the main thoroughfare to Les Halles, and originally the market area dealt in hay, becoming a rest stop for horses. Around 1900, it became *the* market for vegetables.' Marion explains that there was no water in the street when the market started and therefore stallholders did not have the authority to sell meat and fish, just fruit and vegetables. 'The market has been specialising in selling fruit and vegetables ever since,' she says, as we cross over Rue Crozatier.

We turn left down Passage Brulon past sculpture and pottery studios to arrive at the little Square Léo Ferré, which pays homage to the Franco-Monegasque poet and musician. Adjacent is Le Jardin Collectif de la Commune Libre d'Aligre,

Le Jardin Collectif de la Commune Libre d'Aligre

the quarter's communal garden, filled with fruit trees and a rambling potager. A cat snoozes in a puddle of sun. 'The community uses the garden for picnics and fêtes too,' says Diane. 'Our Slow Food association has organised evening *apéritifs* here and we once set up an Aussie barbecue. We had long trestles with a dozen or so salads, a barbecue, and of course a keg,' she laughs.

La Commune Libre d'Aligre is an active association that runs a host of activities and events from political discussions and film screenings to dinners at Café la Commune, in which the Slow Food Movement gets involved. The aim is to promote a spirit of mutual help and camaraderie. Not so long ago the association organised lunch on the Place d'Aligre, where friends and neighbours were encouraged to bring a meal to share. Tables were set up and the day had a Korean cultural focus, with demonstrations and tastings of Korean dishes, dancing, music and art. In the run-up to Christmas, there will be a communal bike ride, where upon completion, participants come together at Place d'Aligre to share *soupe d'oignon*, hot spiced wine and the festive spirit. Those partaking are asked to chop between 1–5 kilos of onions and bring them to Café la Commune on the day. Regularly, in the Café la Commune, local residents put up their hands to cook voluntarily. It could be any number of cuisines from the multicultural population who lives

here. Diane tells me that La Commune provides €200 to produce a meal for up to fifty people, with some produce coming from the communal garden. Guests (it's open to everyone) pay €10 for an entrée, main course and dessert. I am already bowled over by the community feeling in this quarter, *la solidarité*. It's remarkable, and ever so refreshing.

We arrive at the vibrant open-air market on Rue d'Aligre and slip into Sabah on the corner, a crowded North African store bursting with golden saffron, rosewater and red-hot harissa. Next door, aromatic brews float from Café Aouba, where they roast their own coffee. The market is known for its exotic North

African influence (the area became home to immigrants in the nineteenth century), with an enticing synthesis of French and

Arabic cultures. Along with the halal butchers and sacks of couscous you will find Asian and Mediterranean goods. Unusual ingredients are not always easy to find in Paris, so this market is a good bet if you want to prepare an exotic dish with a hit of spice.

We are thrust into the mouth of the market and swept into an intoxicating torrent of colour and culture. Long hair swishes with braids and beads; a red fez hat and a turban bob in front of me. Brown caps of fleshy *cèpes* beg for some garlic. Boisterous stallholders from Algeria, Tunisia and Morocco shout out their wares. It's authentic and alive and while the market is becoming a fashionable place to visit, it stays loyal to its working-class roots. Sunday morning is often the liveliest time to visit food markets in Paris. Marché d'Aligre is no exception – and it offers the added bonus of bargain prices. Keep an eagle eye on what goes in your bag, however. Quality is variable. 'The market is open till half-past one on Sunday,' says Diane, 'and by one o'clock, they're giving stuff away.'

Diane and Marion point things out, and their enthusiasm and attachment to the market are contagious. We pass artichokes and cauliflowers from Brittany, and mounds of brightly coloured chillies. Behind the fruit and vegetable stalls that run down the middle of the road are permanent specialist food shops. Alpage is at number 15. 'An excellent cheese shop and a nice guy,' says Diane. Amira (number 17) sells Algerian pastries and yummy *mihajebs* – soft and stretchy semolina flatbreads stuffed with meat or vegetables. A tempting mid-morning snack. If you'd prefer mint tea with a *beghrir* (a '1000-hole' Moroccan pancake served with a hot butter and honey mixture), go to La Ruche à Miel (honeycomb) at number 19. Paris-Pêche Poissonnerie (also at number 17), is a highly regarded fish store known for its ultra-fresh seafood. It stocks the exceptional fleshy 'oysters Gillardeau', farmed for four generations by the legendary Gillardeau family, a name synonymous with fine oysters. Paris-Pêche has recently opened a little oyster bar a few doors down for those keen to sit and taste their seafood on the spot.

The market flows into Place d'Aligre, punctuated by a small clock tower known as the Notre-Dame d'Aligre. The bell originally rang to herald the opening and closing of the market. On the edge of the square is the renowned Moisan, a fabulous organic bakery filled with rustic Levain rounds, delicious mini raisin and nut breads, and soft viennoises studded with chocolate chips. All of the products are fashioned by hand and of very high quality. There's also an array of tartlets to choose from, squares of pizza, and *ficelles*, small string-like baguettes that are perfect for a morning munch. Today, they come flavoured with cheese, and bacon, or showered in seeds and sea salt.

We enter the Marché Couvert Beauvau-Saint-Antoine, the covered market on the square that has operated for centuries under sturdy wooden beams – a striking architectural feature that resembles an upturned boat hull. It's more gourmet than the open-air market, more stately, and sheltered from the din outside. And there are more oysters. Diane tells me about the traditional oyster lunch the Slow Food Movement put on in honour of the famous epicure Brillat-Savarin, author of the *Physiology of Taste*. 'To celebrate his life,' she says, as she points out the triperie, 'we invited members from around the world to bring a dozen oysters

of their choice. We had a table practically groaning with oysters, as well as the French cheese named after him, of course.'

We poke around. Sur Les Quais, a fine épicerie, holds blind tastings of oils and vinegars. The store specialises in bulk and bottled olive oils from top producers and authentic balsamic vinegar, Aceto Balsamico di Modena, the traditional, aged balsamic made the time-honoured way in the Modena-Reggio region of Italy. Slow food indeed. There's a Portuguese store with custard tarts, Corsican specialty goods, and regional produce from Brittany and the Auvergne. Pommier, a *cave* and gourmet store, specialises in boutique Belgian beers and European micro-brews, with a good selection of raw milk cheeses. In the corner a *cochon de lait* (suckling pig) roasts on a spit.

Flea market, Place d'Aligre

Next, I find myself looking up to a couple of brightly feathered pheasants and an enormous brown hare, hanging from the rafters. Marion and Diane start to tell me about the butcher when a customer joins in. He's a local, a professor of music – jazz, classic, rhythm and blues – and his ancestors are Tuaregs, nomads of the Sahara. 'You meet interesting people like him all the time in the quarter,' says Diane.

Back outside on Place d'Aligre, the flea market is now jumping. Tables overflow with African artefacts, candlesticks and ornate carving sets. Bargain hunters rummage through old vinyl records and bric-a-brac from the dusty attics of Paris. There's even a box of old Michelin Red Guides. Back in the days when the convent Saint-Antoine-des-Champs was in operation, nuns brought old clothes for the poor, and this tradition of recycled clothing

still exists on the square, where you can browse racks of vintage clothing, hats and swathes of embroidered cloth.

The square is surrounded with interesting ethnic stores. Boucherie d'Aligre is a halal butcher that sells beef, veal and lamb. 'There's a huge turnover so you know it's fresh. A lot of the Muslim population in the quarter comes here,' says Diane. Finally, Thailand hits my nostrils: fresh ginger, kaffir lime and coriander in the Asian supermarket.

By 11.45 on this Sunday morning, it's 'madness on market street'. A woman is gathering signatures for a petition and there's a frenetic energy. As the tide of the market recedes, shoppers start to converge on Le Baron Rouge, a rowdy little wine bar with a festive atmosphere, and a local institution. During cooler months and especially at lunchtime on Sundays, it's a magnet for oyster-lovers. Soon, people will be spilling down the footpath sipping a cheery glass of house red and slurping up freshly shucked oysters. There are *rillettes de porc* and cornichons, and simple plates of charcuterie and cheese. Inside, blackboards cover the walls with regional wine offerings. Stuck to the window is a poster for *La Commune* displaying the agenda for forthcoming events. Again, I am struck by the fraternal feeling of this multicultural quarter, the strong glue that holds it together.

Back on Rue de Cotte, Marion and Diane show me La Gazzetta and I peer at the good-value lunch menu on the wall: an assortment of three little tapas entrées; a vegetarian option; and a plate of charcuterie with three entrées du jour. These interesting offerings, quite different from the usual Parisian *formule*, are permanent fixtures on the menu. Swedish chef Petter Nilsson's cosmopolitan cuisine is inventive and market-driven, with lots of lovely vegetables. While I'm studying the menu a man walks by and says, '*C'est très bon ici!*' (It's very good here!). For dinner there is a *prix fixe* menu of three courses for €39 and a *menu carte blanche* for €65. My interest is piqued by the Normandy beef with smoked bone marrow and *l'oignons doux des Cèvennes,* sweet pearly onions that melt in your mouth. These premium onions are grown on terraces by a co-op of small fruit and vegetable producers in the Languedoc-Roussillon region.

Just across the road at number 24 is Retoucherie de Paris. 'This is where I get all my clothes altered,' says Diane. 'The guy is a miracle worker!' Back at our starting point, with a notebook full of treasures, I bid Marion and Diane farewell and walk down Rue Antoine Vollon to join friends for lunch at Le Square Trousseau.

Along the way, I am forced to stop at Blé Sucré. My excuse is that it will be closed by the time I finish lunch. Besides, I've simply heard too much about this tart-box-sized spot to pass without a peek inside. Owned by Fabrice le Bourdat and his wife, this unassuming pastry shop may not garner a second glance from the passer-by but the hint that it's something special is the queue out the door. Like a plain *moelleux au chocolat*, sometimes you have no idea of the pleasure hiding inside until you sink in your spoon and out oozes a molten stream of chocolate lava.

Formerly, the talented le Bourdat was pastry chef at Hôtel Le Bristol's three-Michelin-star restaurant, with a stint at the sumptuous Hôtel Plaza Athénée. My eyes dance from his *mille-feuilles* to the apricot and crumble tarts, to the eye-catching *Saint-Honorés* and sweetest little rhubarb tartlets topped with petals of crisp pastry. They come to rest on his much-talked-about orange sugar-glazed madeleines. I have already tasted that first delicious bite in my mind and breathed in the scent of those tiny sponge cakes mingled with sticky orange icing as I am handed my little sack of four. I reluctantly stash it in my bag for later and push my way out the patisserie door. As well as pastries and gâteaux there is a selection of breads. Prepared sandwiches, quiches and salads can be purchased with a pastry and espresso to enjoy at an

Blé Sucré

Square Frousseau

Le Square Frousseau

vins au verre

Vin de Pays du Gard "Iles Blanches" Viognier 10/11
Chablis *avec* Louis Pière et Fils 10
Sancerre *avec* Florian Mollet 11
Monbazillac *avec* "Roc de Marennes" 08

Vin de Pays d'Oc "Les Crémets" 08/09
Vin de Pays d'Oc "Les Brunes" 08/09
Beaulily *avec* Louis Pière et Fils 10
Sainte Foy Bordeaux *avec* Château Les Hauts de Marne 08/09
Cru Bourgeois Supérieur Médoc *avec* Château Greysac 07

Côtes de Provence *avec* Château d'Esclans "Whispering Angel" 11

coupes et cocktails

Brut Nature Zéro Dosage M. Drappier
Rosé Brut M. Drappier
Carte d'Or Brut M. Drappier
Kir Royal M. Drappier

outside table – or under the trees in the tranquil Square Trousseau across the street, where I hear laughter in the playground and the smack of ping-pong balls.

I follow the trail of crumbs down the street to Le Square Trousseau bistro on the corner. On this chilly day, a couple is lingering over spiced *vin chaud* on the wide, heated terrace. I enter through a plum-coloured velvet curtain into a beautifully preserved Belle Epoque dining room, complete with zinc bar, moulded ceilings, mosaic floor and tulip-shaped light fittings – no doubt the reason this out-of-the-way spot has starred in a number of French films. A table just inside the door displays a beautifully caramelised tarte Tatin and three huge wheels of cheese stacked one upon the other. Already I know what I'm having.

'The discovery of a new dish confers more happiness on humanity than the discovery of a new star.'

JEAN ANTHELME
BRILLAT-SAVARIN

My friends Pam and Mike arrive and we share a bottle of Florian Mollet Sancerre and a board of *saucisson sec de chez Conquet,* accompanied by excellent chewy bread and a dangerously good pat of creamy Beillevaire butter. Pascal Beillevaire's irresistible butter is churned in wooden barrels from rich, raw cream from the Loire, salted with crystals of fleur de sel and moulded by hand. As I am smearing on that butter, I have a déjà vu moment. My grandmother, who made her own blocks of butter in a similar fashion, would have been most impressed.

It's 1 p.m. and guests are streaming in for lunch: a mixed-age, French-speaking crowd. The maître d' is kissing regulars on both cheeks as they arrive, and the young waitresses are all very sweet. The bistro doesn't take bookings but if you arrive by 12.30 p.m. you're almost guaranteed a table. It's a warm, family-friendly place and the park is directly across the road for restless children old enough to play on their own.

Le Square
Trousseau

Soon, diners around me are pulling snails from their shells, eating endives with creamy Roquefort sauce and sliding down half-a-dozen oysters from the French Atlantic Coast. In spring and summer, baked aubergine with mozzarella, artichokes or asparagus tossed in vinaigrette, and tomatoes with melted goat's cheese are on the menu. For main course, I skip the frogs' legs and order a pepper steak with creamy sauce and golden shoestring *frites.* The locals are cutting through juicy steaks and giant cheeseburgers, but there's also risotto and spaghetti on the menu. Pam is enjoying her brochette of prawns with pineapple, coriander and ginger.

Finally, I can order that cheese, their famous farmhouse Saint-Nectaire from the Auvergne. This ancient variety is made from the milk of Salers cows, which graze in the mountains of the region. The three enormous stacked cheeses are brought to my table on a wooden board, and I help myself. It's semi-hard with a dense texture and hazelnut flavour. Chocolate mousse *pour 4 personnes* is being delivered to the table on the right. A *tarte au citron meringuée* to the left. As Pam and Mike linger over *café et petit tiramisu* I tell them about my morning, about the vitality and *solidarité* in this colourful quarter off the beaten track. And then I sit back in this classic Parisian bistro and watch the ebb and flow of lunchtime in Paris with the last of my glass of Bordeaux. What more could you possibly want from a Sunday afternoon? ◊

Summer raspberries at Le Square Trousseau

ADDRESSES

Assaporare
7, Rue Saint-Nicolas, 75012
📞 01 44 67 75 77

Le Baron Rouge
1, Rue Théophile Roussel, 75012
📞 01 43 43 14 32

A la Biche au Bois
45, Avenue Ledru-Rollin, 75012
📞 01 43 43 34 38

Blé Sucré
7, Rue Antoine Vollon, 75012
📞 01 43 40 77 73

La Commune Libre d'Aligre
3, Rue d'Aligre, 75012
www.cl-aligre.org

La Gazzetta
29, Rue de Cotte, 75012
📞 01 43 47 47 05
www.lagazzetta.fr

Marché d'Aligre
Rue d'Aligre, 75012
Métro: Ledru-Rollin
Tuesday–Friday: 8.30 a.m.
to 1 p.m.
Saturday: 8.30 a.m. to 1 p.m.
Sunday: 8.30 a.m. to 1.30 p.m.
Closed Monday

Marché Couvert Beauvau
Hours as above plus 4 p.m.
to 7.30 p.m. Tues–Sat

Le Quincy
28, Avenue Ledru-Rollin, 75012
📞 01 46 28 46 76
www.lequincy.fr

Le Pain au Naturel – Boulangerie Moisan
5, Place d'Aligre, 75012
📞 01 43 45 46 60
www.painmoisan.fr

Slow Food
slowfoodbastille.blogspot.com
www.slowfood.com

Le Square Trousseau
1, Rue Antoine Vollon, 75012
📞 01 43 43 06 00
www.squaretrousseau.com

CHAPTER FOURTEEN

Champagne & TRUFFLES

◆◆◆

'Where shall we go for lunch?' I ask my dear friends Grahame and Pierre. Always the first and most important question! Epicures with a taste for the finer things in life, they throw around a few options before deciding on **Les Tablettes de Jean-Louis Nomicos.** 'Nomicos has launched out on his own,' says Pierre. 'He was previously running the kitchen at Lasserre and we've heard very good things about his new restaurant in the 16th. He has an extraordinary lunch menu for €58.' Le Menu Club Dans les Tablettes comprises a choice of an entrée, a main course, cheese, dessert, coffee and half a bottle of wine. I can't imagine who would say no to such an offer!

We make a date for lunch and on a crisp winter's day, sit down in a dining room that's full of sunshine. It happens to be the last day of my trip and a lovely farewell. The contemporary décor is light and cheerful, with orange banquettes and glassware, and wicker basket walls, a setting true to Nomicos' Mediterranean roots. It's a smart French clientele: suits in their lunch break and well-dressed couples. The appealing short menu changes frequently with both the seasons and the chef's desires, and is presented to us in an envelope, conjuring an element of anticipation and surprise. Pierre requests the wine list and is given an iPad. He chooses a region and then the wine. This imaginative concept, from which the restaurant takes its name, Les Tablettes, also provides diners with details of produce and producers, creating a deeper understanding and appreciation of the dishes. An idea, I am sure, that will spread like hot butter in a pan.

We choose from four entrées and four main courses and after a tantalising *amuse-bouche* of *royale de foie gras et mousse*

de lentilles with a *réduction de porto chutney de vinaigre* served in a little glass pot, I enjoy a velvety Jerusalem-artichoke soup with flavoursome *cèpe* wontons and parsley jus. It's chic and contemporary but with a feeling of generosity. Grahame and Pierre opt for the beautifully presented *fois gras de canard* with fruit, port, ginger and *pain d'épice.* Shaped by excellent training, this is well-executed, serious cooking that's also creative. When Nomicos was just eighteen he went to work for Alain Ducasse at the luxury Hôtel Juana in the Mediterranean resort of Juan-Les-Pins, and by his late twenties became executive chef at La Grande Cascade in the Bois de Boulogne, a luxurious, Belle Epoque restaurant in the woods on the fringe of the 16th. His refined technique and modern take on classic dishes at Lasserre earned him two Michelin stars.

Four Seasons
George V

Inspired by memories of his rural childhood, Nomicos has a deep respect for the seasons and his cooking evokes the flavours and spirit of the South of France. For main course, a brandade of fresh cod is served with marjoram, black olives and a capsicum confit. Grahame savours his *cuisse de lièvre effilochée*, shredded leg of hare in a rich sauce with gnocchi and chive butter. On the à la carte menu is Nomicos's signature macaroni with black truffles and foie gras, a reinterpretation of a recipe by Auguste Escoffier – more reason to return.

While we eat, I ask Grahame and Pierre about their favourite gastronomic restaurants in Paris. 'Le Meurice,' says Pierre without hesitation, 'it's right across the road from the Jardin des

Tuileries, where the French play pétanque.' 'And Carré des Feuillants,' says Grahame. The three-Michelin-star Le Meurice in the luxurious palace hotel is certainly an address to remember for a very special occasion. Modern French cuisine is served in the seventeenth-century dining room. Literally around the corner, Alain Dutournier, chef-owner of the contemporary two-star Carré des Feuillants, is known for his original and surprising cuisine.

Cheese is next. I am excited to see that today's *affiné du moment* is a rich and luscious Brillat-Savarin, a triple-cream, melt-

in-the-mouth Brie that sits at the top of my list of favourite French cheeses. It is, as expected, addictive. For dessert, we linger over pink grapefruit with a hibiscus *gelée* and lime and vanilla sorbet. It's refreshing, tangy and interesting. Time always seems to scoot by when you're enjoying yourself, and suddenly I'm in danger of being late for my next delicious rendezvous! We throw back our coffees, accompanied by three precious little pastries presented like stars on a stage, and jump in the car. I'm sure it won't be long before we see a Michelin star here too.

Pierre skilfully navigates his way around the busy Place Victor Hugo and cuts through to the Four Seasons George V in the heart of the glitzy Golden

Four Seasons
George V

Triangle. Tasteful white fairy lights shower the beguiling façade behind the line-up of luxury cars. There is a flurry of goodbyes and swiftly I am ushered into a mythical world of grace and elegance.

Impossibly beautiful, this glorious hotel is everything you'd dream of if Paris were to be poured into a single luxurious package, and a gorgeously gift-wrapped one at that! The iconic address, which is among France's grandest hotels, is known to locals simply as Le George V. Warm and romantic, the lobby and public areas are sights to behold, decorated with bold, fresh blooms inventively arranged in oversized glass vessels. The hotel's signature floral displays are created inhouse by artistic director Jeff Leatham and his team, with nine thousand blooms delivered weekly from the Netherlands. Famous around the globe, the flowers alone are worth a visit.

Four Seasons George V

Right now, however, it is not flowers that are on my mind, but chocolate. I am accompanied down to the hotel's spa for my much-anticipated rendezvous, gliding over Italian marble past a forest of sparkling Christmas trees in the courtyard. A harp plays in the background. The ambience of the hotel is magical and already I feel spoiled. As I round a corner, my eyes fall on a tranquil pool stretching into the distance, surrounded by misty trompe l'œil murals evoking the gardens of Versailles. While the pool is for hotel guests only, the comprehensive menu of (regally priced) spa treatments is available for all, and popular with Parisians. I sit and relax with a tisane in the lounge watching the water gently lap. The spa was designed to conjure up an eighteenth-century Versailles feel, and the walls and chairs are covered in pretty Toile de Jouy fabric. Amongst the Spa Journeys is a 'Jet Lag Recovery' package, ideal for lagging travellers in need of

a pick-me-up, and the signature treatment is 'A Stroll Through Versailles'. Aided by music of the era, guests are taken back in time to experience two and a half hours of pampering inspired by the beauty regime of the queen herself. This delicious indulgence begins with an orange blossom scrub and ends with pink pastries. My extravagance today, however, is the decadent one-and-a-half-hour chocolate treatment, 'All About Chocolate', a divine way to wind down a busy trip to Paris.

I slip into a soft, fluffy robe in the opulent changing rooms, pretending I'm Marie Antoinette in her boudoir, before greeting Dominique. She tells me she has been a masseuse here since it opened in 1999 and before that, at the Ritz. 'Hotel spas have taken a while to catch on in Paris,' she says. 'Once Le George V created a spa, Le Meurice and Hôtel Plaza Athénée followed suit.'

Four Seasons
George V

The first step is an invigorating chocolate body scrub, designed to exfoliate and energise. Then, refreshed from a shower, I watch Dominique beat melted chocolate in a bowl. She holds up the spoon and it falls back in a velvety ribbon. 'The perfect consistency,' she declares. I sink into the table as warm, molten chocolate is massaged into my skin. Like drinking hot chocolate at bedtime, there is a calming effect, almost soporific. It's soothing and nurturing and smells heavenly. At this moment, I could stay here forever cocooned in chocolate, insulated from the world. Alas, the chocolate starts to dry and I am woken from my reverie to wash it all down the drain once more in preparation for the final stage of the treatment. The last step is a deep tissue massage with warm shea butter. Those aching muscles, the consequence of running around Paris with a heavy bag, fade away and my skin feels as smooth and silky as chocolate. I finish, *bien sûr,* with a few exquisite truffles.

Now that I'm relaxed, it is time for a leisurely afternoon tea. All of the city's luxury hotels offer tea, but it's hard to beat Le George V. Firstly, the welcoming Galerie that faces on to an interior garden courtyard has bags of charm, with elegant classical furniture, Flemish tapestries and those breathtaking blooms again. Today it is decorated festively for Christmas. Secondly, there is the tea itself, served from 3 p.m. to 6 p.m. For a decadent indulgence, *Thé Complet à la Française,* the full French-style tea, entices visitors with three tiers of treats that involve savoury delicacies and miniature French pastries with a pot of tea, coffee or hot chocolate and a glass of bubbly for €55. It's a wonder-

Four Seasons
George V

fully lavish way to celebrate a special occasion and to experience a blissful Parisian setting without breaking the bank. Alternatively, there's a classic English afternoon tea (*sans* Champagne), and also *un chariot de pâtisserie* or menu for those who would rather choose one perfect pleasure. In summer, the courtyard, transformed with flowers, provides an outdoor alternative for tea or an *apéritif,* as well as lunch and dinner.

I sip Champagne and chat with Caroline, the charming young director of public relations of the hotel. I ask Caroline, a chic woman who has lived in Paris all her life, about her favourite places to visit in the city. 'Le Bon Marché department store – it's more traditional and classic than the others, chic and elegant,' she says.

'I adore Le Musée de la Vie Romantique with its *petit jardin*, and the Jacquemart-André. As for restaurants, Guy Savoy has Les Bouquinistes on the river opposite Le Pont Neuf, and Atelier Maître Albert.' This contemporary rôtisserie near Nôtre Dame has an open fire and specialises in spit-roasted farmhouse chicken, meats and fish: perfect for a cold night. 'Oh, and you can't miss the President Wilson market. The George V buys some of its produce there; the quality is excellent.'

We pause in our conversation as that irresistibly seductive dessert trolley is wheeled to our plush seats, filled with classic French pastries. Everything is made inhouse and on top of the trolley is a plantation of adorable, king-size raspberry lollipops with fresh raspberry centres. The only difficult decision of the afternoon is what to choose! I eventually decide on a chocolate *religieuse,* a kind of éclair cake, consisting of a small cream puff placed on a larger one, both filled with pastry cream and topped with chocolate icing, in keeping with this afternoon of chocolate.

'And of course there are the beautiful Palais Royal gardens,' Caroline continues. 'If you cross to the Left Bank from here you can picnic on the Pont des Arts.' This pedestrian bridge over the Seine has become *un pique-nique* destination.

'Great love affairs
start with Champagne
and end with tisane.'

HONORE DE BALZAC

I watch hot chocolate being served from a silver *chocolatier* as dainty tiered plates of afternoon tea float by. 'The Galerie has become *the* elegant spot, where a lot of Parisians come,' explains Caroline. Locals are also rather fond of the hotel's two-Michelin-star restaurant Le Cinq, where chef Eric Briffard has been at the helm since 2008. He hails from Burgundy, where his grandparents' farm gave him an early understanding and appreciation of seasonality and fresh ingredients, while his stint in Japan shows up subtly in his modern

French cuisine. Currently the winter menu highlights pearly scallops from the Baie de Seine, blue lobster and black truffles, along with Briffard's speciality, 'luscious poached Bresse Miéral hen served with whole vegetables, a suprême truffle sauce and stuffed cabbage in a spicy consommé.' There are 50 000 bottles in the cellar while a separate *cave* keeps one hundred varieties of Champagne perfectly chilled.

'You must go to Christmas carols in one of the cathedrals, and to the Christmas market on the Champs-Elysées near the Rond-Pont,' says Caroline. Coincidentally, I had walked that way this morning, past the village of white wooden huts selling everything from mulled wine and gingerbread to crêpes and grilled salmon sandwiches. Carollers give the village a festive atmosphere. I love Paris in the wintertime. With the fantastical displays in the department store windows, twinkling trees and roasting chestnuts, there's an extra layer of glamour and enchantment. 'Also near the Rond-Pont is Le Mini Palais,' says Caroline. 'Eric Fréchon is the consulting chef and there's a gorgeous outdoor terrace.'

Darkness blankets the city by the time we finish tea, and outside, tiny white lights sparkle down the avenue. In the heart of a neighbourhood dripping with style, the hotel is surrounded by exclusive designer boutiques for that last, caution-to-the-wind splurge. It's also dashing distance to the Seine, where I blow a kiss goodbye to the Eiffel Tower, glowing softly in the twilight.

I rush back to the Marais, pack and change before my long flight home. It is 8 p.m. I sip tea and peer out of the window one last time, watching life on the street below. In the apartments opposite, tables are being set for dinner and wine is being poured amid a warm, golden glow. On the footpath, Sébastien is waiting beside his vintage Peugeot. It's not until I collapse into my plane seat that I realise my skin is still perfumed with chocolate. In fact, the delicious scent is positively wafting through my pores. ◊

HÔTEL LE BRISTOL >>

I simply can't sign off before talking about my other favourite luxury hotel. **Le Bristol** may be a palace (the first French hotel, in fact, to obtain the 'Palace distinction' in 2011), but it's also family-friendly with its very own cat! Fa-raon, an affectionate, fluffy Birman, recently celebrated his second birthday. This lucky cat has the run of the place, dining on scraps from Eric Fréchon's recently refurbished three-Michelin-star restaurant and sleeping beside the switchboard. Last I saw him he was snoozing on a table in the hotel's breathtakingly beautiful garden. There are rules, however. He is allowed everywhere but the restaurant, kitchen and bedrooms. For the equally fortunate children who stay here, the hotel provides an all-year-round kids' program, with an egg hunt at Easter time, Christmas activities and a big magical tree that lights up the garden.

The French-style garden happens to be my all-time favourite spot in Paris for a stylish cocktail in summer, and the restaurant also spills into the garden when it's sunny. However, you must book, even for an *apéro*, if the weather is fine. In inclement weather, the garden is closed. It's a great spot for people-watching and a popular Parisian meeting place at any time of the day. At tea time, you can indulge in a classic English-style afternoon tea.

The hotel is located on the elegant Rue du Faubourg Saint-Honoré, a legendary street for shopping, and has been welcoming privileged guests since 1925. The 188 rooms and ninety-two suites are gorgeous, and were originally private apartments, bought one by one. The last of the residents lived in an operating hotel. Every room is different and all have been recently renovated, decorated in classic eighteenth-century style. The large Paris Suite has its own steam room and view of the Eiffel Tower, while the penthouse looks down to the garden and has four connecting bedrooms and two private terraces. There is always a celebrity or two staying at the hotel, particularly from the cinema world, and the penthouse is a favourite haunt of the Jolie-Pitt clan. There is a rooftop pool and a brand-new spa, which won the prize for 'Best New Luxury Spa in the World' at the World Luxury Spa Awards 2012, while Le 114 Faubourg, the hotel's luxury brasserie, received its first star in the 2013 Michelin guide.

The hotel puts on a monthly Fashion High Tea, where you can sip tea and Champagne and pick at perfect pastries while models parade around the bar past enormous bouquets of pink and white hydrangeas. Recently, I joined a bevy of excited little girls in party dresses with their mothers and grandmothers for a peek at the latest children's collections from Stella McCartney.

Next time I visit Paris, I want to stay at the Bristol!

Hôtel Le Bristol | 112, Rue de Faubourg Saint-Honoré, 75008 |
☎ 01 53 43 43 00 | www.lebristolparis.com

ADDRESSES

Atelier Maître Albert

1, Rue Maître Albert, 75005
☎ 01 56 81 30 01
www.ateliermaitrealbert.com

Les Bouquinistes

53, Quai des Grands Augustins, 75006
☎ 01 43 25 45 94
www.lesbouquinistes.com

Carré des Feuillants

14, Rue Castiglione, 75001
☎ 01 42 86 82 82
www.carredesfeuillants.fr

Four Seasons George V

31, Avenue George V, 75008
☎ 01 49 52 70 00
www.fourseasons.com/paris

Le Mini Palais

3, Avenue Winston Churchill, 75008
☎ 01 42 56 42 42
www.minipalais.com

Restaurant Le Meurice

228, Rue de Rivoli, 75001
☎ 01 44 58 10 55
www.lemeurice.com

Les Tablettes de Jean-Louis Nomicos

16, Avenue Bugeaud, 75016
☎ 01 56 28 16 16
www.lestablettesjeanlouisnomicos.com

ACKNOWLEDGEMENTS

To all those who worked so hard to bring this delicious project together, *merci beaucoup*! The route along the way has been like scooting around the Arc de Triomphe at night: always exhilarating, sometimes challenging and occasionally daunting, but Lantern was always there to shine a bright light and steer me in the right direction.

A heartfelt thank you to the entire team at Lantern, a group of tremendously talented and lovely people who have guided me along the way with enthusiasm, patience and unfailing encouragement. You are all an inspiration.

A special thank you goes to my publisher Julie Gibbs, not only for her unwavering faith and confidence in the project, but for allowing me to follow my heart with a large dollop of freedom. To Publishing Manager, Katrina O'Brien, thank you for shaping *Delicious Days* into a truly beautiful book.

Jocelyn Hungerford has been such a delight to work with and I shall miss our communications. Nothing was too much trouble as she calmly and elegantly edited the manuscript – tolerating my finicky suggestions and giving me reassurance when I needed a lift. Gifted designer Emily O'Neill breathed life into my words and astounded me with her fresh approach and creativity, while still staying open to my ideas. Her quirky hand-drawn maps add another layer of interest and excitement to the book, as do Amy Golbach's adorable illustrations, scattered like pleasant little surprises throughout the pages.

A sincere thank you to Emirates for providing flight support, and *merci mille fois* to Peter and Lesley Thomas, dear and generous friends who offered me their beautiful apartment in the Marais while researching the book, an utterly delightful haven to relax and tap away in.

What would I have done without the goodwill of my wonderful friends in Paris? I am ever appreciative of photographer Vincent Bourdon who, out of the goodness of his heart, zoomed around town on his *moto* to take beautiful shots of Paris for me. As always, Grahame Elliott and Pierre Fontaney got straight on task when I asked them a favour from afar, calling up on my behalf to check obscure but necessary details. I owe the breathtaking shot of the dancer taken at Académie Américaine de Danse de Paris to Vincent Desnoës, and to Jocelyn McGinnis – thank you for your company. We always have a great time researching when I'm in town!

To the owners of all the pâtisseries, boutiques, restaurants, confiseries and chocolate shops who allowed me into their worlds, and to photograph inside their premises, I thank you, along with all those kind souls who offered their goods and services on a complimentary basis. Sébastien Bazin, chauffeur extraordinaire, saw to it that a car was on my doorstep whenever I needed one and went out of his way to show me 'his Paris'. I enjoyed a morning dipped in chocolate with Context Travel and a day cycling around the countryside courtesy of Fat Tire Bike Tours. The Trianon Palace dished up a lovely lunch on the terrace and Le George V spoiled me with afternoon tea and a decadent chocolate massage, a relaxing and welcome treat at the end of a hectic research trip.

Back in Adelaide, a special thank you to my ever-dependable old friend David Smith who came to the rescue and wrestled with my out-of-control file of shots, putting them in a dignified order and patiently helping me to choose a final selection. To all of my friends at home – *merci* for your ongoing support and encouragement.

Lastly, and most importantly, my biggest thank you is to my family, who are there for me *toujours*. I am especially grateful to my two gorgeous girls, Georgie and Annabelle, who have endured the creation of another book with grace (most of the time!). Annabelle took on the role of walking-French-dictionary and grammar guru, while Georgie became my go-to-girl when I needed a chapter read and an honest opinion. Thank you to the moon and back for your love and support. I could never have done it without you.

LANTERN

Published by the Penguin Group
Penguin Group (Australia)
707 Collins Street, Melbourne, Victoria 3008, Australia
(a division of Penguin Australia Pty Ltd)
Penguin Group (USA) Inc.
375 Hudson Street, New York, New York 10014, USA
Penguin Group (Canada)
90 Eglinton Avenue East, Suite 700, Toronto, Canada ON M4P 2Y3
(a division of Penguin Canada Books Inc.)
Penguin Books Ltd
80 Strand, London WC2R 0RL England
Penguin Ireland
25 St Stephen's Green, Dublin 2, Ireland
(a division of Penguin Books Ltd)
Penguin Books India Pvt Ltd
11 Community Centre, Panchsheel Park, New Delhi – 110 017, India
Penguin Group (NZ)
67 Apollo Drive, Rosedale, Auckland 0632, New Zealand
(a division of Penguin New Zealand Pty Ltd)
Penguin Books (South Africa) (Pty) Ltd, Rosebank Office Park, Block D,
181 Jan Smuts Avenue, Parktown North, Johannesburg, 2196, South Africa
Penguin (Beijing) Ltd
7F, Tower B, Jiaming Center, 27 East Third Ring Road North,
Chaoyang District, Beijing 100020, China

Penguin Books Ltd, Registered Offices: 80 Strand, London, WC2R 0RL, England

First published by Penguin Group (Australia), 2014

3 5 7 9 10 8 6 4

Cover design by Emily O'Neill © Penguin Group (Australia)
Text design and maps by Emily O'Neill © Penguin Group (Australia)
Illustrations by Amy Golbach
Photographs on pages ii, vii, 18, 228, 232, 233, 234, 235 & 236 by Guillaume de Laubier (GV hotel); pages viii, 9, 10, 208, 223 (all) &
224 (all) by Vincent Bourdon; page 183 (dancer, top right) by Vincent Desnoës; pages 13, 64, 88 (blossoms, top right), 108, 113, 145
(sweets, top right), 150 & 183 (dancer's feet top left) by Shutterstock; and pages 34, 46, 80, 94, 116, 138, 162 & 176 by Getty Images.

Every effort has been made to contact the copyright holders. In cases where efforts were unsuccessful,
the copyright holders are asked to contact the publisher.
All meals, accommodation and other travel expenses were paid for by the author unless otherwise stated.

Typeset in Calluna by Post Pre-Press, Brisbane
Colour separation by Splitting Image Colour Studio, Clayton, Victoria
Printed and bound in China by 1010 Printing International Limited

National Library of Australia
Cataloguing-in-Publication data:

Paech, Jane, author.
Delicious days in Paris/Jane Paech.
9781921383045 (paperback)
Includes index.
Paris (France) – Description and travel.
944.084

ISBN 9781921383045

penguin.com.au/lantern